SHORT & SWEET

SHORT & SWEET

SOPHISTICATED DESSERTS IN 30 MINUTES OR LESS

MELANIE BARNARD

PHOTOGRAPHS BY ANN STRATTON

HOUGHTON MIFFLIN COMPANY

BOSTON   NEW YORK

FIRST HOUGHTON MIFFLIN PAPERBACK EDITION 2007

Visit our Web site: www.houghtonmifflinbooks.com.

The Library of Congress has cataloged the hardcover edition as follows:

Barnard, Melanie.

Short and Sweet : sophisticated desserts
in no time at all / Melanie Barnard.
p. cm.
ISBN 0-395-90145-6
1. Desserts.   2. Quick and easy cookery.   I. Title.
TX773.b365   1999
641.8'6—dc21   99-12463   CIP

ISBN-13: 978-0-618-87269-5 (pbk.)
ISBN-10: 0-618-87269-8 (pbk.)

Book design by Anne Chalmers
Typeface: Adobe Garamond and Copperplate

Food Styling by Rory Spinelli and Roscoe Betsill
Prop Styling by Robyn Glaser

Printed in the United States of America
DOW 10 9 8 7 6 5 4 3 2 1

FOR MOM

When I was a child, my mother baked every single day, and there was always a full-fledged dessert at the dinner table. Coming home from school, I would sniff and try to guess just what it was that she had spent the morning making. If you think that my mind is playing tricks on me and that no mom like this ever really existed outside of television, ask anyone who lived on Gordon Lane in Erie, Pennsylvania, in the fifties and sixties. Mom had such a reputation for brownies that they were requested at my thirty-fifth high school reunion. Her spice cake with seafoam frosting is in its second generation as a top birthday choice, and people still comment on her cherry pies, though she maintains to this day that she never could get the filling quite right. My mother baked for love.

This book is for you, Mom. You *did* get the filling right.

ACKNOWLEDGMENTS

More than any book I've ever written, this one was just plain fun. And no wonder: imagine waking up in the morning and knowing you'll spend the day eating tarts and cookies and hot fudge sundaes! Not surprisingly, this project drew many willing tasters.

Tasting, of course, was just the beginning. I'm especially grateful to everyone who helped me. Thanks to:

Rux Martin, for believing that we all need a little dessert in our lives, and for her kind, witty, and sharp editorial eye.

Lori Galvin-Frost, whose constant watch over the book made it the best it could be.

Anne Chalmers, for creating a book design of real beauty.

Ann Stratton, whose imaginative photographs showcase the desserts, and to Rory Spinelli, Roscoe Betsill, and Robyn Glaser, the stylists who made them look so good.

Jayne Yaffe, who clarified, quantified, and made everything clearer.

Rose Grant, whose competent indexing makes the book thoroughly usable.

Isabelle Vita, for her trusted checks and balances.

Deborah DeLosa, for loving and promoting well beyond the call of duty.

Judith Weber, my agent, whose support keeps all my soufflés rising high.

Mary Faso, my sister, who is not only my best friend, but my most honest, vigilant, and enthusiastic recipe tester.

Brooke Dojny, my longtime writing partner and friend, for her unfailing generosity in spirit, and the sharing of her recipes.

My husband, Scott, my three sons, and my daughter-in-law, who put up with my sweet nothings every day.

With all of you, life is a delicious dessert. Thank you.

Contents

INTRODUCTION

I'll never give up dessert. Not ever. A fudgy brownie with a glass of cold milk, a slice of warm apple pie with a wedge of cheddar, a mound of ice cream melting under rivulets of warm butterscotch sauce, or a slice of feathery layer cake with dollops of whipped cream are simply too much a part of my life to relegate to memory alone.

Like my mother and my grandmother before her, I know that a cake or pie cooling on the counter is a guarantee that the family will be on time for supper. My schedule no longer allows for all-day bake-a-thons, but lack of time isn't stopping me from serving dessert every day. I still make crisps and cobblers, pies and cookies, mousses and soufflés, and fabulous candies. I've found ways to prepare them in a fraction of the time they used to take.

Short & Sweet is about delicious simplification. With these recipes, you can make utterly irresistible desserts from just a few ingredients—no more than seven—and have them on the table in short order, almost always in less than half an hour. There are no gimmicks or tricks. Like all good recipes, the ones in this book depend solely on excellent ingredients and sound techniques.

Choosing the right ingredients always makes a critical difference in both time and taste. Even the most sophisticated chocolate truffles require nothing more than chocolate, cream, and a little flavoring. A splash of aged balsamic vinegar on ripe strawberries sends the flavor soaring. When you start with perfectly ripe pears, all you have to do to put a classic Italian dessert on the table in less than five minutes is add a drizzle of anise liqueur, a bit of Parmesan cheese, and a grinding of black pepper. Using sweetened condensed milk ensures that fudge will turn out smooth and silken every time, with no need for split-second timing or an intimidating candy thermometer.

Proper handling can turn a mediocre fruit dessert into a memorable one. Store-bought apricots release sunny flavor when they're poached in a good wine, while plums can be brought to juicy perfection in just a few minutes with gentle braising. Roasting peaches, pears, or rhubarb intensifies their natural sweetness.

Some of the quickest and easiest desserts of all

are traditional ones. Many people think the first step in making butterscotch or chocolate pudding is opening a box of dusty-tasting mix, never dreaming that an infinitely better homemade version takes one additional minute to stir together. Fruit fools, swirls of pureed fruit and whipped cream, have unlimited flavor possibilities and are mindlessly simple. The billowy French and Italian custards known as sabayons and zabagliones whip up in just 10 minutes, rising to elegance with the aid of nothing more than a whisk and a saucepan. The most impressive dessert of all, the soufflé, is only an illusion of difficulty: in reality, it's no more than egg whites and yolks distinctively flavored with fruit, chocolate, liqueur, or a combination of the three.

Years of experience have taught me how to take nips and tucks to streamline preparation time. Traditional recipes for cookies have you soften the butter to room temperature before using a mixer to beat it with sugar, a step that's time-consuming, messy, and sometimes totally unnecessary. Often, all you have to do is to melt the butter in a saucepan, dump in the remaining few ingredients, and stir with a wooden spoon. No sifting flour, no beating butter, and no washing bowls and beaters.

This "melt-add-stir" technique saves at least 15 minutes and can be used for bar cookies, shortbreads, and drop cookies. Even simple cakes like gingerbread and crumb cake take easily to the one-pan method, and both are so moist and filled with spicy fragrance that they don't need any frosting.

Time-saving desserts often have cleaner, more vibrant flavors than their elaborate predecessors. Eliminating the egg-yolk custard in chocolate mousse, for example, highlights its suave decadence that is its *raison d'être*. Likewise, puffed peach soufflé doesn't need the conventional custard base because pureed dried peaches provide ample support and sing with ripe peach flavor.

Perhaps my most important realization has been that I no longer have to make every single thing from scratch. Fifty years ago, my Sicilian grandmother, a busy woman who knew the value of convenience products well before her time, created a signature layered dessert in about five minutes from vanilla ice cream, crumbled store-bought biscotti, and dried fruits soaked in liqueur. Palermo Parfaits remain a family favorite.

Following in her footsteps, I take advantage of the high-quality refrigerated pie crusts, puff pastry, and phyllo dough that are available. With them, I can make pies and tarts in fewer than 30 minutes, including baking time. Store-bought pound and angel food cakes become memorable when filled with jams or preserves, prepared lemon curd, or chocolate-hazelnut spread. The premium ice creams on the market beg to be instantly personalized with homemade sauces like hot fudge or butterscotch.

Now no matter how busy I am, I never need to sacrifice dessert. And with these recipes, you won't have to either.

The Short & Sweet Basic Pantry

**IF YOU HAVE MOST OF THESE THINGS
ON YOUR SHELF OR IN YOUR REFRIGERATOR OR FREEZER,
YOU CAN ALWAYS MAKE A GREAT DESSERT.**

The Shelf

*(Read labels: some products must be refrigerated after
opening.)*

ALMOND PASTE, CANNED

BAKING SODA AND BAKING POWDER

CHOCOLATE: bittersweet, unsweetened, semisweet,
German's, white, chocolate chips

CHOCOLATE PETIT FOUR OR TART SHELLS (found in
candy stores and in many supermarkets in the
candy section)

CHOCOLATE WAFER COOKIES, such as Nabisco Famous Wafers

CHOCOLATE-HAZELNUT SPREAD, such as Nutella
(found near the peanut butter in many supermarkets)

CITRUS CURD, lemon and/or lime (found in the supermarket near the jams and jellies)

COCOA POWDER, unsweetened, preferably European-style

COCONUT, shredded sweetened

CORN SYRUP, light and dark

DRIED FRUITS, such as raisins, currants, mixed
chopped fruit, cranberries, cherries, and figs

FLAVORING EXTRACTS (vanilla, almond), pure

FLOUR, all-purpose

FRUIT PRESERVES, JAMS, AND MARMALADES

FRUIT SYRUPS (found in coffee shops and in some
supermarkets near the cocktail mixes)

GINGERSNAPS

GRAHAM CRACKERS

HONEY

LIQUEURS AND LIQUORS: coffee-, anise-, raspberry-,
and orange-flavored; rum and bourbon

MAPLE SYRUP

MARSHMALLOW FLUFF

MOLASSES

NONSTICK OIL SPRAY

NUT BUTTERS: smooth or chunky peanut, cashew, almond (found near the peanut butter in many supermarkets)

NUTS, such as chopped skinned hazelnuts, peanuts,
almonds, pecans

SPICES: cinnamon, cloves, ginger, allspice, mace

SUGAR: granulated, powdered, light and dark brown

WINES, such as marsala, dry white, dry sherry

THE REFRIGERATOR

BUTTER, preferably unsalted

CITRUS FRUIT, lemons, limes, oranges

CREAM, heavy

CRÈME FRAÎCHE (found in the dairy section of some supermarkets and in specialty stores)

EGGS, large

HALF-AND-HALF

MILK, preferably whole

PIE CRUSTS, refrigerated folded (found with the refrigerated cookie and biscuit doughs in the supermarket)

SOUR CREAM

YOGURT, plain or flavored

THE FREEZER

ICE CREAM: vanilla, chocolate, coffee

PHYLLO DOUGH AND SHELLS

POUND CAKE

PUFF PASTRY SHEETS

EQUIPMENT WORTH HAVING

BAKING DISH, Pyrex (8-by-8)

BAKING PANS, metal (8-by-8, 9-by-9, 7-by-11, 9-by-13)

BAKING SHEETS, shiny aluminum (buy good-quality ones that won't warp)

CHERRY PITTER (you'll use it only three months out of the year, but you'll love it)

CITRUS ZESTER (costs about $5.00 and worth every penny)

CUSTARD CUPS (5-, 6-, and 8-ounce)

DOUBLE BOILER (or a bowl that fits into a saucepan to make a double boiler)

ELECTRIC MIXER, best-quality hand-held (you usually get what you pay for)

FOOD PROCESSOR

GRATER, four-sided

MEASURING CUPS, liquid and dry (get both)

MEASURING SPOONS

MICROWAVE OVEN (a small one will do a good job of melting chocolate and butter)

MIXING BOWLS, set of three (glass can go in the microwave, but metal is best for whipping cream)

MUFFIN TINS, standard and miniature

NUTMEG GRATER

PAPER DOILIES for dusting powdered sugar or cocoa designs on unfrosted cakes

PIE PLATE, Pyrex (9-inch)

SCALE (not strictly necessary but very helpful)

SPATULA, rubber

SPOON, wooden

STRAINER, medium-sized, aluminum or stainless steel

TARTLET PANS (4½-inch), with removable bottoms

TART PAN (9-inch), metal, with removable bottom (makes a tart look very professional)

TIMER (if you don't have a good one on the stove)

WHISK

The Secrets of Sweet Success

Dairy Products and Eggs

Most dairy products, especially cream for whipping, should be kept in the coolest part of the refrigerator, usually in the back. The door, often the designated dairy place in newer refrigerators, is actually the warmest, and thus worst, place to store milk and cream.

Heavy cream works better for whipping than products labeled "whipping cream." Pasteurized, but not "ultrapasteurized," cream seems to whip a bit higher and thicker, but the latter is easier to find, less expensive, keeps longer, and works just fine, too.

Unsalted butter is best for desserts. It usually has a sweeter, more buttery flavor and seems firmer and richer than its salted counterpart. That said, these recipes work fine with salted butter if that is what you have on hand. *Do not substitute margarine or vegetable shortening.* They sometimes give unexpected results and react very differently from butter in many baked goods.

Eggs should be stored in their original container in the back of the refrigerator for maximum coolness and minimal temperature flux. Do not transfer them to those cute little plastic egg holders in the door. Rather, use the holders for storing jars of condiments that would otherwise get lost on the shelf.

Separating egg yolks from whites is best accomplished while the egg is still cold from the refrigerator, when the yolk and white are most firm. Crack the egg against the side of the bowl, allowing the white to drop into the bowl, while slipping the yolk back and forth between the two pieces of shell.

Room-temperature egg whites beat faster and higher than cold whites. To beat, start on low speed until the clear, viscous liquid becomes a white froth. Then increase the speed to medium-high. When the whites look like soft clouds, add sugar slowly and continue to beat just until the whites are glossy, moist, and hold peaks when the beater is lifted.

Low-fat dairy products, such as cream or ricotta cheese, ice cream, and milk, will work as substitutes for full-fat products in most recipes. Never substitute nonfat dairy products. For maximum flavor and texture, I usually cook with full-fat dairy products, though I do prefer to drink low-fat milk.

FRUITS AND NUTS

FRESH FRUIT loses flavor as soon as it is refrigerated, no matter what anyone tells you. Buy fruit as close to ripe as you can, then keep it on the counter and use it as soon as it is ready. You can chill citrus fruits, but keep them in the fruit drawer or near the front of the refrigerator, where the temperature is a few degrees warmer than in the back. I keep apples in my garage (the modern equivalent of a root cellar). If you live in a hot climate, your air-conditioned house is probably cooler than the garage.

For CITRUS PEEL AND JUICE, grate the peel before juicing the fruit, and use only the colored part; avoid the white pith, which is bitter. Choose lemons, limes, and oranges that feel heavy for their size, as they will probably give more juice and have thinner skins.

Use a four-sided grater for finely grated citrus peel. Use a "citrus zester" tool to make long, thin shreds. A "citrus reamer," which looks like a zester but has a single, larger hole, is used to make slightly wider strips.

To get the maximum amount of juice, a few seconds in the microwave oven will warm up even the chilliest lemons, limes, or oranges.

NUTS AND NUT BUTTER should be refrigerated once they have been opened to preserve freshness and keep natural oils from quickly turning rancid. Unopened jars or cans can be kept in a cool pantry.

LIQUID FLAVORINGS

LIQUEURS, LIQUORS, AND WINES add distinctive, sophisticated flavor and often additional sweetness to many desserts. Because the quantity of liquid may be crucial to the success of a recipe, they cannot always be omitted, but nonalcoholic liquids can often be substituted.

FLAVORING SYRUPS are a fine nonalcoholic substitute for liqueurs in most recipes. You can find them in bottles at most boutique coffee shops and many supermarkets.

EXTRACTS, especially vanilla and almond, are important dessert shelf staples. Pure extracts are more costly than artificially flavored ones, but are worth every penny.

EQUIPMENT

LIQUID AND DRY MEASURING CUPS are different from each other, so be sure to use the right one for the designated ingredient.

OVENS have their own personalities, hot spots, temperature fluctuations, and temperaments. It is well worth the investment of a few dollars to buy an oven thermometer. If it registers more than 25 degrees off the mark, call a serviceman. If the variation is less than 25 degrees, make the appropriate adjustment yourself when you set the temperature dial.

PASTRY

Puff pastry, phyllo dough, and pie crusts are easiest to use if well chilled. All will have optimal flakiness if kept cold right up until they're ready for baking. A few minutes in the freezer while the oven preheats works wonders.

AND FINALLY . . .

Unlike most cookery, baking is a science that requires a certain degree of precision and timing. So, while you can fudge the amounts and ingredients in a fruit compote, you must follow the directions precisely when making a chocolate soufflé, or you might end up with a fallen fudge brownie—a fine thing in itself, but not what you had in mind.

A Quick Chocolate Primer

All chocolate desserts, especially those with few other ingredients, depend both on the chocolate itself and how it is treated by the cook.

Choosing Chocolate

Read the labels on the package, looking for cocoa butter and no other fat, real vanilla and not artificial vanillin. Lecithin is OK; it's often added to chocolate as a natural stabilizer and emulsifier, and it does not affect the taste. But chocolate brands do have distinct flavors. Fine-quality cooking chocolate and chocolate chips are produced in the United States by Nestlé, Hershey, Baker's, and Ghirardelli. Imported chocolates that are especially good for cooking include Lindt, Callebaut, Perugina, and Valrhona.

UNSWEETENED CHOCOLATE (bitter or baking chocolate) contains 100 percent cocoa liquor and should have no sugar added.

BITTERSWEET and the slightly sweeter SEMISWEET chocolate have varying amounts of sugar added. They are usually interchangeable in recipes, and in this book can be used either in the form of chocolate chips or bar chocolate. Note that 1 cup of chocolate chips equals 6 ounces of bar chocolate.

SWEET CHOCOLATE, most commonly sold as German's Sweet Chocolate (so-called because it was invented by a man named Samuel German), has more sugar as well as lecithin and other flavors added.

MILK CHOCOLATE has a higher percentage of milk solids and sugar than semisweet.

UNSWEETENED COCOA has some of the cocoa butter pressed out. It can be purchased both as standard American (widely distributed by Hershey) and European-style, or "Dutched," cocoa, which has been processed with alkali to reduce bitterness. European, or alkalized, cocoa is imported but is also now produced by Hershey in America.

WHITE CHOCOLATE is not considered real chocolate. It is called confectionery coating or white chips or white baking bars. In this book, white chips and baking bars are interchangeable. One cup of white chips weighs 6 ounces. Be sure to buy only high-quality white chocolate (I like Ghirardelli, Lindt, and Nestlé) because cheap brands may not melt and mix well.

When working with chocolate, there are a few important things to know:

•Chocolate chips do not lose their shape during melting, so don't be fooled into overheating them. Simply stir the chocolate to smooth it out.

•If you melt chocolate in a microwave oven, read the directions for your appliance, then run a few test melts, as each oven operates slightly differently.

•If you melt chocolate in the top of a double boiler, be sure that no water or steam comes in contact with the chocolate, or it might "seize" and turn into a totally unworkable solid mass. The chocolate can be reliquefied by adding a very small amount of vegetable oil, but it still may not work well in recipes.

•Always remove chocolate from the heat before it is completely melted. Then stir until it is melted and smooth. This gentle melting method reduces the risk of burning and helps to cool the chocolate more quickly so it can be added to other ingredients, such as whipped cream or eggs.

•If melted chocolate is too hot, it will immediately turn solid when it comes in contact with the cold ingredients, such as cream. If it is too cold, of course, it will solidify on its own.

•Store chocolate in a cool, dry place. Temperature fluctuations will cause it to develop a grayish cast, or "bloom." Flavor, however, is not affected and the bloom disappears upon melting.

TOPPING IT OFF: WHIPPED CREAM BASICS

Many an otherwise exemplary dessert has been ruined by a squirt of canister whipped topping. Once you understand how to whip cream properly, you will never be content with anything else. The secrets are few:

♦ Use heavy cream—whipping cream does not have as high a butterfat content, and thus deflates more quickly and easily.

♦ Old-fashioned pasteurized heavy cream will whip thicker and higher than the newer "ultrapasteurized," but it has a much shorter shelf life, so be sure to check the expiration date.

♦ Put the cream, beaters, and mixing bowl in the freezer for 5 to 10 minutes before whipping. This chilling time results in fluffier, more stable whipped cream.

♦ Use a metal bowl for whipping, as it gets colder faster and stays colder than glass or plastic.

♦ Whip just until the peaks stand up by themselves when the beaters are raised; overwhipping causes unsightly grainy clumps.

BASIC SWEETENED WHIPPED CREAM

MAKES ABOUT 2 CUPS

1 cup chilled heavy cream

2 tablespoons granulated or powdered sugar

½ teaspoon vanilla extract

If using an electric mixer, start whipping the cream with the sugar on medium-low speed until the cream thickens. If you plan to serve the whipped cream within an hour, use granulated sugar. If you want to refrigerate it for up to 3 hours, use powdered sugar, which has a touch of cornstarch to help stabilize the cream. Add the vanilla, then gradually raise the speed of the mixer until the cream reaches firm peaks. Watch it carefully so it doesn't overwhip and begin to turn grainy.

If using a whisk, just keep whisking!

Add after the cream has thickened:

- **COCOA CREAM:** 2 tablespoons European-style unsweetened cocoa and 1 additional tablespoon sugar

- **CAPPUCCINO CREAM:** 2 teaspoons instant espresso or coffee powder

- **FLOWER WATER CREAM:** 2 teaspoons orange flower water or rose water, plus 2 tablespoons chopped edible flowers, such as organic pansies or violets (optional)

- **SPICED CREAM:** ¼ teaspoon ground ginger, cardamom, cloves, mace, or freshly grated nutmeg

- **CHOCOLATE CREAM:** 2 ounces semisweet or white chocolate, melted and cooled to tepid. Add when cream has whipped to soft peaks. Do not overbeat or the cream will become grainy.

- **CITRUS CREAM:** 1 teaspoon grated orange, lemon, or lime peel

- **SPIRITED CREAM:** 1 to 2 tablespoons liqueur to taste

COOL FRUITS

FROM EARLIEST RECORDED HISTORY, MANKIND HAS LOVED FRUIT. AFTER ALL, EVE didn't reach for a green bean. It was the apple that caught her eye, and ever since that first fall, we've been tempted by whatever fruit happens to be in season.

When I was a child living on the fertile shores of Lake Erie, we marked the seasons by the fruit and vegetable crops as they "came in." June began with strawberries, July followed with cherries, and in August, we had bumper crops of peaches and plums. An extensive grape harvest and apple picking took place right up until the first frost. We never ate these fruits out of season, and we eagerly anticipated each one. Lush, ripe fruits were always given star treatment, with very few embellishments.

This less-is-more concept is the inspiration for many of my fruit desserts. Simply splashing a little balsamic vinegar over strawberries heightens their flavor. Macerating melons in grappa is a classic Italian way to bring out the best in them.

Of course, supermarkets carry apricots in December and grapefruit in July. All this out-of-season convenience comes at a price—both in dollars and in taste. Fresh fruits should be purchased at their peak, although some, such as pears and bananas, will continue to ripen on the countertop. Buy berries and summer stone fruits ripe and eat them within a day or two. Avoid refrigerating fruit, as the chill halts the ripening process and also begins to turn natural fruit sugars into other less tasty starches.

"To everything there is a season," and flavor is the reason why it's best to serve strawberries in spring and melons in summer, rather than the other way around. I sometimes think Eve's greatest failing might have been that she just didn't have the patience to wait.

Chocolate-Dipped Strawberries with Mint Cream

4 SERVINGS

STRAWBERRIES, ESPECIALLY the giant, long-stemmed varieties, don't require peeling, pitting, or even stemming. The natural sweetness of good strawberries in season—and they are rarely naturally sweet out of season—pairs perfectly with slightly bittersweet chocolate. This showy, sophisticated springtime dessert takes about 15 minutes to prepare. Serve it after a very special dinner or nibble it with a cup of afternoon tea.

Rinse the berries, then pat completely dry on paper towels. Line a small baking sheet with waxed paper. In a small saucepan set over hot water or in a custard cup in a microwave oven, melt the chocolate. Dip each berry into the chocolate to cover at least half. Set the berries on the waxed paper. Refrigerate for about 10 minutes to set the chocolate. (The dipped berries can be then held at room temperature for up to 2 hours.)

Whip the cream with the powdered sugar and crème de menthe or mint extract to firm peaks. (The cream can be whipped up to 3 hours ahead and refrigerated.)

Make a bed of mint sprigs on a small platter or make separate beds on 4 individual dessert plates. Set the berries on the mint, then spoon a dollop of the whipped cream alongside them. Dip the berries into the cream and enjoy.

16 large strawberries, preferably with stems

4 ounces bittersweet chocolate, coarsely chopped

1 cup heavy cream, chilled

¼ cup powdered sugar

2 tablespoons white crème de menthe or ¼ teaspoon mint extract

1 bunch fresh mint, separated into sprigs

STRAWBERRIES IN BALSAMIC PEPPER SYRUP

6 SERVINGS

5 tablespoons honey

3 tablespoons balsamic vinegar

¼ teaspoon coarsely ground black
    pepper

1 pint strawberries, hulled and halved

1 large, firm banana, peeled and sliced

In a medium mixing bowl, whisk the honey and vinegar until well
blended. Stir in the pepper. Add the strawberries and stir gently to
coat with the syrup. Let stand for 5 to 10 minutes at room temperature. Stir in the banana. Serve the fruit and syrup in shallow dessert
bowls or stemmed goblets.

CHOCOLATE-MARSHMALLOW STRAWBERRY DIP

4 SERVINGS

In a small saucepan, stir the cream and chocolate over medium-low heat until the chocolate is melted. Remove from the heat and stir until smooth. Stir in the marshmallow fluff until blended and smooth. Let cool until lukewarm, about 10 minutes. (The sauce can be refrigerated for up to 24 hours, but return to room temperature for serving.)

To serve, divide the sauce among 4 small custard or dessert cups. Place the cups in the center of 4 dessert plates and surround with the berries for dipping.

THOUGH PALE COCOA IN color, this fluffy sauce has a surprisingly intense bittersweet chocolate flavor. Because it is thick, it coats the strawberries nicely, and it's a particularly quick and easy way to showcase the long-stemmed strawberries that often appear in the supermarket in May and June. If they are not available, use large, flavorful strawberries and toothpicks for dipping.

½ cup heavy cream

2 ounces (2 squares) unsweetened chocolate, coarsely chopped

2 cups marshmallow fluff

20 large strawberries with stems or 2 pints large strawberries and toothpicks

RASPBERRIES IN CHAMPAGNE

4 SERVINGS

4 tablespoons honey, preferably berry-blossom honey

3 tablespoons raspberry liqueur, such as Framboise

2 tablespoons lemon juice

3 tablespoons chopped fresh mint, plus 4 sprigs for garnish

1 pint fresh raspberries, preferably a mix of golden and red berries

2 cups chilled champagne

In a small saucepan, heat the honey, liqueur, lemon juice, and chopped mint just until smooth. Remove from the heat and let steep for 10 minutes. Strain out the mint. (The syrup can be used immediately or refrigerated for up to 6 hours.)

Divide the raspberries among 4 champagne flutes. Pour the syrup over the berries, then pour in the champagne. Garnish with mint sprigs. Serve immediately.

Raspberries in Chantilly Cream

4 SERVINGS

THIS SIMPLE DESSERT highlights elegant raspberries in three ways. The fresh berries are served over sweetened whipped cream that has been flavored with both raspberry preserves and raspberry liqueur. Offer thin, crisp sugar cookies or chocolate wafers as a pleasing crunchy contrast to the soft pink cloud in each bowl.

Whip the cream with the jam, powdered sugar, and liqueur until it's thickened and forms very soft peaks. (The cream can be prepared up to 2 hours before serving and refrigerated.) Divide the cream among 4 shallow dessert bowls. Sprinkle ½ cup of berries over the top of each. Serve immediately.

1 cup heavy cream, chilled

¼ cup seedless raspberry jam

¼ cup powdered sugar

1 tablespoon raspberry liqueur, such as Framboise

2 cups fresh raspberries

NANA, MY SICILIAN grandmother, used grappa, a smooth brandy from Italy, to complement the heady cantaloupes and the mature mint from her late-August garden. I've tried the dessert with other brandies and any combination of melons that are available. Nana, who was as pragmatic about her cooking as she was about life, would approve. To speed up the preparation further, you can buy sliced melon at the supermarket salad bar.

1-2 lemons

⅓ cup grappa or other brandy

¼ cup superfine granulated sugar

3 tablespoons slivered fresh mint, plus sprigs for garnish

4 cups sliced summer melon, such as a mixture of cantaloupe, honeydew, and Persian melon (don't use watermelon)

MIXED MELONS IN GRAPPA

4 SERVINGS

Use a small sharp knife or a zester to cut 1 tablespoon thin strips from the colored part of the lemon peel. Squeeze 2 tablespoons lemon juice. In a shallow dish, such as a glass pie plate, stir together the lemon peel, juice, brandy, sugar, and 2 tablespoons of the mint. Add the melon slices and stir gently to coat. Cover and refrigerate for at least 15 minutes or up to 1 hour.

To serve, arrange the melons in overlapping slices (vary the colors if using more than one variety of melon) on 4 dessert plates. Stir the remaining 1 tablespoon of mint into the macerating liquid and spoon it over the melon slices. Garnish each serving with a mint sprig.

Sweet Watermelon "Salsa" with Sugared Tortilla Chips

4 SERVINGS

Preheat the oven to 400 degrees. Place the tortillas on a baking sheet. Sprinkle each evenly with 1 tablespoon of the sugar. Use a sharp knife or pizza cutter to cut each tortilla into 6 wedges. Bake until tortillas are crisp, golden, and glazed with melted sugar, 5 to 8 minutes. (The tortilla chips can be baked up to a day ahead and stored in an airtight container.)

Grate 1 teaspoon of the colored part of the peel and squeeze 1 tablespoon juice from the lime.

In a mixing bowl, stir together the watermelon, chopped mint, tequila or orange juice, remaining 1 tablespoon sugar, lime peel, and juice. Let stand at least 15 minutes or refrigerate for up to 4 hours before serving.

To serve, spoon the salsa and any juices into a pretty bowl, and garnish with mint sprigs. Spoon the yogurt into another bowl. Serve with the sugared tortilla chips for dipping.

THIS INVENTIVE RECIPE CAN be easily doubled or tripled and served in hollowed-out cantaloupe, honeydew, or even a small watermelon, depending upon the size of the group and the amount you make. It is a particularly good recipe for beach or backyard picnics because no plates or utensils are needed. Replace the tequila with orange juice, and it's a great summer Sunday breakfast or brunch offering as well.

Because underripe watermelon can be watery and flavorless, be sure to choose fruit that is fully ripe, deep red, and fragrant.

4 (8-inch) flour tortillas

5 tablespoons granulated sugar

1 lime

4 cups coarsely diced watermelon (about 1 pound)

⅓ cup chopped mint, plus sprigs for garnish

¼ cup tequila or orange juice

1 cup lemon yogurt

Apricots with Ricotta Cream

4 SERVINGS

Sweetened ricotta spiked with anise and studded with nuts and dried fruits is a classic cannoli filling. The filling itself is a breeze to make, but spooning it into the cannoli shells is tedious and time-consuming. This cream is a nice counterpoint to fresh apricots. Serve crisp cookies, such as Italian pizzelles or amaretti, on the side for a pleasant contrast in texture.

2 tablespoons pine nuts

1 cup ricotta cheese

¼ cup powdered sugar

2 tablespoons anise liqueur, such as Sambuca, or ¼ teaspoon anise extract

¼ cup chopped mixed dried fruits

4 large or 8 small apricots, pitted and thickly sliced

Toast the pine nuts in a dry skillet over medium heat, stirring, until golden and fragrant, 2 to 3 minutes. Immediately remove them from the skillet to prevent burning. (Or toast on a small baking sheet in a 375-degree oven, stirring once or twice, for about 5 minutes.) In a food processor, puree the ricotta, powdered sugar, and liqueur or extract until very smooth. Add the dried fruits and process just until combined. (The cream can be prepared several hours in advance and refrigerated.)

To serve, spoon the cream into the center of 4 shallow dessert dishes. Sprinkle with the pine nuts. Arrange the apricot slices around the cream.

APRICOTS AND FLOATING FLOWERS

4 SERVINGS

I DEVELOPED THIS SIMPLE compote in the late summer, when my nasturtium pot was overflowing with bright, peppery flowers. Other unsprayed edible blossoms, such as marigolds or roses, can also be floated in the fruit. Peaches or plums can stand in for the apricots.

Grate 1 teaspoon of the colored part of the peel from the lemon and squeeze 2 teaspoons juice. In a deep bowl, stir together the lemon peel and juice, marsala, and sugar until the sugar is dissolved. Add the apricots, stirring gently. Let stand for 15 minutes at room temperature or refrigerate for up to 2 hours, stirring several times. Return to room temperature before serving.

Meanwhile, toast the almonds in a dry skillet over medium heat, stirring constantly, until golden and fragrant, about 3 minutes. Immediately remove them from the skillet to prevent burning. (Or toast on a small baking sheet in a 375-degree oven, stirring often, for about 5 minutes.)

Just before you are ready to serve, thinly slice 1 of the flowers and stir into the apricot mixture. Serve the fruit and liquid in bowls and sprinkle with the toasted almonds and garnish with the remaining whole flowers.

1 lemon

½ cup marsala

2 tablespoons granulated sugar

6 fresh apricots, pitted and quartered

¼ cup sliced almonds

5 organic nasturtium or other edible flowers

THESE STUFFED FIGS ARE sophisticated little sweets to enjoy with espresso. Mascarpone is readily available, but if you can't find it, substitute 5 ounces softened cream cheese mixed with ¼ cup sour cream. Pitted apricots can be stuffed with the mixture as well.

Chopped skinned hazelnuts are readily available, and they are a real timesaver. If you elect to skin your own, first lightly toast them for 5 to 8 minutes in a 375-degree oven, then rub the warm nuts in a cloth dish towel to remove most of the skins, which are slightly bitter.

¼ cup chopped skinned hazelnuts

6 ounces (¾ cup) mascarpone cheese

¼ cup powdered sugar

¼ teaspoon ground cinnamon

8 large or 12 small fresh figs

2 tablespoons Frangelico or brandy

STUFFED FIGS

4 SERVINGS

Toast the hazelnuts in a small dry skillet over medium heat, stirring, just until they begin to color and are fragrant, about 2 minutes. (Or toast them on a small baking sheet in a 375-degree oven, stirring once or twice, for about 5 minutes.) Immediately transfer the nuts to a small plate and let cool.

In a small bowl, blend together the cheese, powdered sugar, and cinnamon.

Cut a deep slit in each fig and squeeze it gently to open the fig. Spoon about 1 tablespoon of the mascarpone into each fig, then sprinkle the cheese with the hazelnuts. Set the figs on a small dessert platter and dribble the Frangelico or brandy over them. Serve immediately.

MIXED BERRY CHAMPAGNE GAZPACHO

4 SERVINGS

LIGHT AND REFRESHING, THIS fruit soup is wonderful on a summer evening, especially following a substantial supper of grilled steak and potatoes. Angel food cake "croutons" add the perfect crunch. To keep the bubbly in the soup, assemble it at the last minute. It takes no time.

Preheat the oven to 400 degrees. Cut the cake with a serrated knife into ¾-inch cubes. Place on a baking sheet and toast in the oven, stirring once or twice, until golden brown and crisp on all sides, 5 to 8 minutes. (The cake croutons can be made a day ahead and stored in an airtight container.)

In a food processor, puree the strawberries in the syrup. Add the champagne and blend briefly. Ladle the soup into 4 shallow bowls. Sprinkle with the mixed berries and cake croutons. Dollop with the yogurt or crème fraîche. Serve immediately.

3 ounces purchased angel food cake (about one-fourth of a 10- or 12-ounce cake)

1 (10-to-12-ounce) package frozen strawberries in light or heavy syrup, nearly thawed

1½ cups champagne, chilled

1½ cups mixed fresh summer berries, such as raspberries, blueberries, or blackberries

½ cup vanilla yogurt or crème fraîche

PEARS WITH PECORINO AND PEPPER

4 SERVINGS

Grate about 2 teaspoons of the colored part of the peel from the lemon and squeeze 2 teaspoons juice.

Overlap the pear slices on each of 4 dessert plates. Sprinkle with the lemon juice and the grated peel. Stir together the liqueur or syrup and honey, then drizzle over the pears. Scatter the cheese shavings over the pears and grind about ⅛ teaspoon pepper over each serving. Serve immediately.

1 lemon

4 ripe pears, peeled and sliced

4 tablespoons Strega or Sambuca or anise liqueur, or anise syrup

2 tablespoons honey

1½ ounces shaved pecorino cheese (about ⅓ cup)

½ teaspoon coarsely ground black pepper

COOL POACHED PEARS WITH SHAVED CHOCOLATE

4 SERVINGS

It's difficult to find a good pear anymore. Though they are usually rock-hard when picked and shipped to market, pears do ripen well on the counter. It's tough to predict which pear will develop a lush perfumy fragrance and buttery texture, and which one will get soft and grainy. Fortunately, even imperfect pears are redeemed by poaching. Because they are among the sweetest of fruits, they are a natural counterpoint to dark bittersweet chocolate. You can, of course, make your own chocolate sauce (see page 84), but a good chocolate bar shaved over the top of the pears will do just fine.

In a small saucepan just large enough to accommodate the pears, bring the wine, sugar, ginger, cinnamon stick, and ½ cup water to a boil over medium-high heat. Add the pears (the liquid may not totally cover them), reduce the heat to medium-low and cover the pan. Poach, gently turning the pears several times, until just fork-tender, about 15 minutes. Use a slotted spoon to remove the pears from the poaching liquid and place in a shallow dish or bowl.

Boil the poaching liquid, uncovered, until reduced by about one-third, about 5 minutes. Pour over the pears and cool in the refrigerator for at least 10 minutes or up to 3 hours, removing them from the refrigerator at least 15 minutes before serving.

To serve, place the pears in 4 shallow dessert dishes. Spoon about 3 tablespoons syrup over each pear. Use a swivel vegetable peeler or small knife to grate long shards of chocolate over the dessert.

1½ cups dry white wine

½ cup granulated sugar

4 tablespoons chopped candied ginger

1 cinnamon stick, broken in half

4 small ripe but firm pears, such as Comice or Anjou, peeled and cored

1 bittersweet chocolate bar (2-3 ounces)

SOUTHERN PINEAPPLE-CITRUS SALAD

6 SERVINGS

¼ cup sliced almonds

¼ cup bourbon or orange juice

3 tablespoons honey

½ teaspoon curry powder

3 cups sectioned mixed grapefruit and
    oranges

2 cups fresh pineapple chunks

1 cup red seedless grapes

Toast the almonds in a dry skillet over medium heat, stirring, until golden brown and fragrant, 2 to 4 minutes. Immediately remove them from the skillet to prevent burning. (Or toast on a small baking sheet in a 375-degree oven, stirring occasionally, for about 5 minutes.)

In a 2-quart glass bowl, blend together the bourbon or orange juice, honey, and curry powder. Add the grapefruit and oranges, pineapple, and grapes and stir to mix. Refrigerate for at least 15 minutes or up to 2 hours.

Just before serving, sprinkle the fruit with the toasted almonds.

CLEMENTINES IN MULLED-WINE SYRUP

4 SERVINGS

CLEMENTINES, A CROSS between Mandarin and Seville oranges, have a flavor reminiscent of tangerines, but without the pesky seeds. They are abundant in the market during the winter holidays.

Use a small sharp knife to score the peel of 1 of the clementines or oranges into quarters. Remove the colored part of the peel and cut it into thin strips less than ¼ inch wide, or dice coarsely into ¼-inch pieces. Peel the other 3 fruits completely, discarding the peel.

Place the strips of orange peel, the wine, sugar, mulling spices, and lemon juice into a small nonreactive saucepan. Bring to a boil, stirring to dissolve the sugar. Boil the mixture gently for about 4 minutes, until it is slightly reduced.

Lightly pull apart the fruit so that the sections form a sort of petal shape. Place the fruit in individual shallow dessert dishes. Pour the hot syrup and spices over the fruit. Let stand about 15 minutes at room temperature before serving, or refrigerate for up to 2 hours, removing from the refrigerator 15 minutes before serving.

4 large clementines or small seedless oranges

1 cup port wine

½ cup granulated sugar

1 tablespoon "mulling" spices, or a mixture of 6 whole cloves, 6 whole allspice berries, and 1 cinnamon stick, broken

2 tablespoons lemon juice

ORANGE AND GRAPEFRUIT COMPOTE WITH CANDIED ZEST

4 SERVINGS

3 seedless oranges

2 grapefruit, preferably Texas "ruby reds"

⅓ cup granulated sugar

2 tablespoons Triple Sec or other orange liqueur, or frozen orange juice concentrate, thawed

Use a small knife or zester to remove the colored part of the peel of 1 of the oranges and 1 of the grapefruits. Cut enough of the peel of each fruit into thin strips no more than ¼ inch wide to measure about 1 tablespoon each. Squeeze the juice of the peeled grapefruit and orange to measure about ¼ cup each.

Place the peel in a small nonreactive saucepan and cover with water by 1 inch. Bring to a boil, reduce the heat to medium and simmer, uncovered, for 5 minutes. Drain in a small sieve and discard the liquid. Return the peel to the saucepan, along with the sugar and both citrus juices. Bring to a boil, stirring to dissolve the sugar, then reduce the heat to medium-low and simmer, uncovered, until the peel is translucent and the syrup is thickened, 7 to 10 minutes. Remove from the heat and stir in the liqueur or concentrate. (The syrup and peel can be refrigerated for up to 2 days. Return to room temperature, and thin with a little orange juice if necessary.)

Meanwhile, peel the remaining grapefruit and 2 oranges, then cut crosswise into ½-inch-thick slices. Cut each slice in half and arrange them in overlapping circles on each of 4 dessert plates or on a single platter. Pour the syrup and candied peel over the fruit. Serve at room temperature or lightly chilled.

CITRUS PLATTER WITH GINGER-WHITE CHOCOLATE SAUCE

4 SERVINGS

In a small bowl set over a pan of simmering water or in a microwave oven, gently heat the chocolate until it is nearly melted (about 1 minute in the microwave). Remove from the heat and stir until smooth. Let cool for 2 minutes. Gently stir in the sour cream and ginger until blended, then stir in the liqueur or syrup. (The sauce can be refrigerated for up to 3 days. Rewarm very gently before using.)

Arrange the fruits on each of 4 dessert plates. Spoon the warm sauce over the fruit.

MOST SUPERMARKET SALAD bars and produce sections sell sliced or sectioned grapefruit and oranges. Pink grapefruit makes a lovely addition to the mix, and other tropical fruits, such as bananas, pineapples, papayas, or kiwis, can be incorporated if they are available. The sharp flavor of freshly grated ginger plays well against the sweetness of white chocolate in this warm sauce.

6 ounces (1 cup) white chocolate chips or chopped white chocolate bar

3 tablespoons sour cream, at room temperature

2 tablespoons grated fresh ginger

1 tablespoon ginger or orange liqueur, or orange or maple syrup

4 cups sliced or cut-up mixed citrus fruits, such as oranges, tangerines, and grapefruit

Tangelos in Warm Caramel Sauce

4 SERVINGS

5 tangelos or seedless oranges

⅔ cup packed light brown sugar

⅔ cup dry white wine

1 tablespoon chopped fresh rosemary or 1 teaspoon dried

2 bay leaves, broken in half

2 tablespoons B&B liqueur

Use a small sharp knife or zester to make thin shreds of the colored part of the peel of 1 of the tangelos or oranges, then squeeze about ⅓ cup juice from the fruit. In a medium nonreactive saucepan, bring the peel, juice, brown sugar, wine, rosemary, and bay leaves to a boil, stirring to dissolve the sugar. Simmer the mixture over medium heat until it is reduced by about one-third and syrupy, 8 to 10 minutes. Stir in the liqueur.

Meanwhile, peel the remaining 4 tangelos or oranges, discard the peel, and cut the fruit crosswise into slices about ½ inch thick. Arrange in 4 shallow dessert dishes or a rimmed platter. Remove the bay leaf from the syrup and ladle over the fruit. Serve immediately or refrigerate for up to 1 hour before serving.

SLICED KIWIS AND PAPAYAS WITH RUM SAUCE

4 SERVINGS

ASIAN DESSERTS ARE OFTEN light, fruity, and presented with as much whimsy and imagination as the rest of the meal. In this one, kiwis and golden papayas complement each other, and the fruit pieces are spread over the alternating fruit purees, while macadamia nuts add a rich, salty crunch. The result is strikingly colorful and takes only minutes to prepare.

Peel the fruits and scoop the seeds from the papayas. Slice 1 of the papayas and 2 of the kiwi fruits and reserve. Cut the remaining papaya into chunks and puree in a food processor, along with 1½ tablespoons of the sugar, 1 tablespoon of the rum or orange juice, and 1 teaspoon of the lemon juice. Transfer to a small bowl.

Puree the remaining 2 kiwis with the remaining 1½ tablespoons sugar, 1 tablespoon rum or orange juice, and 1 teaspoon lemon juice. (The sauces can be covered and refrigerated for up to 8 hours.)

To serve, spread the papaya sauce over half of each of 4 dessert plates. Spread the kiwi sauce over the other half of the plates. Arrange the sliced fruits over the opposite sauces. Sprinkle with the macadamia nuts.

2 large ripe papayas

4 kiwi fruits

3 tablespoons granulated sugar

2 tablespoons golden rum or orange juice

2 teaspoons lemon juice

¼ cup chopped macadamia nuts

SUGARY RIPE PAPAYAS ARE perfectly balanced by a sweet-tart syrup, which is given a kick by jalapeño peppers.

PEPPERED PINEAPPLE PAPAYAS

4 SERVINGS

¼ cup frozen pineapple juice concentrate, thawed

¼ cup golden rum or orange juice

1 tablespoon lime juice

1 small jalapeño pepper, seeded and minced

⅓ cup pecan pieces

2 papayas, peeled, seeded, and sliced

In a small bowl, whisk together the pineapple juice concentrate, rum or orange juice, lime juice, jalapeño, and 2 tablespoons water. Refrigerate for at least 10 minutes or up to 2 hours. Toast the pecans in a dry skillet over medium heat, stirring, until a shade darker in color and fragrant, about 3 minutes. Immediately remove them from the skillet to prevent burning. (Or spread on a small baking sheet and toast in a 375-degree oven, stirring occasionally, for 5 to 8 minutes.)

To serve, arrange the papayas in overlapping slices on 4 dessert plates. Drizzle with the pineapple syrup, and sprinkle with the nuts.

MANGO-COCONUT CREAM SOUP

4 SERVINGS

CANNED CREAM OF COCONUT isn't just for piña coladas anymore. Pureed with mango and white wine, it makes the easiest and fastest soup in the Caribbean. A few gingersnaps on the side provide a nice crunch.

Toast the coconut in a dry skillet over medium heat, stirring, until golden brown and fragrant, 2 to 3 minutes. Immediately remove it from the skillet to prevent burning. (Or toast on a small baking sheet in a 375-degree oven for 3 to 5 minutes, stirring occasionally.)

In a food processor, puree the mangoes, then add the wine and cream of coconut. Process until smooth. (The soup can be prepared 2 hours ahead and refrigerated.)

To serve, ladle into shallow dessert bowls. Sprinkle with the toasted coconut.

¼ cup shredded sweetened coconut

2 mangoes, peeled and cut into chunks

1 cup dry white wine, chilled

½ cup canned sweetened cream of coconut

Montego Bay Mangoes

4 SERVINGS

Though I first tasted these mangoes as part of a Caribbean breakfast, the combination is much too good to be relegated to morning. The sweetness of the fruit and the rich tartness of lime-spiked crème fraîche provide a marvelous finish to a spicy jerked pork or chicken barbecue.

Admittedly, mangoes take a bit of time to prepare because the flesh clings stubbornly to the inner seed. But the flavor is well worth the effort, and the rest of the dessert goes together in a flash.

2 limes

2 mangoes, peeled and sliced

4 tablespoons golden rum or orange juice

¼ cup crème fraîche

2 tablespoons powdered sugar

Grate 1 teaspoon of the colored part of the peel from 1 of the limes and squeeze 1 tablespoon juice. Cut 4 thin slices or wedges from the remaining lime.

Arrange the mangoes in overlapping slices on 4 dessert plates. Drizzle with the rum or orange juice and sprinkle with the lime juice. In a small bowl, blend together the crème fraîche, powdered sugar, and lime peel. Spoon in ribbons over the mangoes. Garnish with the lime slices and serve.

HARLEQUIN FRUITS

4 SERVINGS

THE SUCCESS OF THIS ultraeasy confection depends on the quality of both the dried fruits and the chocolate. Choose moist, plump fruits. For the chocolate, indulge in your favorite specialty brand. Because you can keep all the ingredients on hand in your cupboard, this is the perfect sweet to serve when unexpected guests come for coffee.

Melt the chocolates separately in small saucepans set over hot water, or in small bowls in a microwave oven (30 to 45 seconds in a microwave). Line a small baking sheet with waxed paper.

Using a toothpick or your fingers, dip the fruits into the chocolate, one piece at a time. Or you can dip each piece into one chocolate only, or dip each fruit halfway into each chocolate so that one end of each fruit is white and one is dark for a harlequin effect. Or dip the fruits in one chocolate until nearly covered, then use a fork to drizzle the other chocolate over the dipped fruit. (The fruits can be stored at room temperature in a tightly covered container for up to 2 days.)

3 ounces bittersweet or semisweet chocolate, chopped

3 ounces white chocolate, chopped

16 dried fruits, such as apricots, figs, pears, apples, peaches, or prunes

TUSCAN ROSEMARY AND PINE NUT BARS

PAGE 152

DOUBLE CHOCOLATE PUDDING
PAGE 131

BLUEBERRY CORN CAKE

PAGE 174

RASPBERRY LEMON LAYER CAKE
PAGE 193

STRAWBERRIES
IN BALSAMIC PEPPER SYRUP
PAGE 26

WARM MOCHA TRUFFLE CAKE
PAGE 188

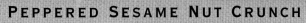

PEPPERED SESAME NUT CRUNCH
PAGE 217

WHIPPED CHOCOLATE TRUFFLES   CHOCOLATE THIN MINT TRIANGLES
PAGE 223   PAGE 220

SCOTCH BUTTERSCOTCH SAUCE
PAGE 82

WARM FRUITS

THE REFRIGERATOR IS A WONDERFUL INVENTION, BUT NOT FOR FRUIT. IF YOU'VE ever ripened a couple of peaches, pears, or mangoes to peak perfection on your countertop, eaten one immediately and stuck the other in the drawer of the fridge for even a few hours, you'll know what I mean. The glacial chill of the refrigerator acts like a killer frost. The fruit's texture, which was at first as smooth as butter, is now grainy, and the full-bodied perfume has vanished. In-season fruit from your local farmstand tastes better than any that you buy in the supermarket, not just because it was freshly picked, but also because it has not been refrigerated.

Indeed, I've occasionally considered how I might feel after having traveled 20 hours in the cargo hold of an airplane, another 8 hours in the back of an 18-wheeler, more time on a loading dock, then a couple of days in a walk-in refrigerator. I might like a warm bath. That is exactly why gentle heating can do wonders for fruit that has not been given time to come to full flavor—the only kind that most of us can get during much of the year.

Poaching or braising in a warm, aromatic liquid infuses the fruit with enough sweetness to bring out its natural sugars and reinvigorate its flagging spirits. Conveniently, poached and braised fruit can usually be cooked ahead, chilled, and then reheated for serving, because cooked fruit doesn't seem to suffer from the cold shoulder as raw fruit does.

Grilling or roasting also produces spectacular results in minutes. The high, dry heat acts like a shot of adrenaline for fruit, especially when it is already fresh and flavorful. The natural sugars caramelize and intensify and the fruit takes on a rich color.

The chemistry of cold and its numbing effects on flavor explain why fruit should never be refrigerated for more than a couple of hours. For perfection, warming is usually the best way to go.

ROASTED RHUBARB

4 SERVINGS

EVEN BRIEF COOKING WITH sugar turns rhubarb into a rosy-blushed, soft, sweet-tart compote that is good warm, cool, or chilled. The traditional cooking method is to stew the fruit in a little liquid and sugar, but roasting gives it an even more intense flavor.

Preheat the oven to 450 degrees. Grate 1 teaspoon of the colored part of the peel from the orange and squeeze ¼ cup juice.

In a shallow 2-quart baking dish, stir together the rhubarb, sugar, ginger, orange peel, and juice. Spread evenly in the dish. Bake, stirring 3 or 4 times, until the rhubarb is soft, but retains its shape, about 25 minutes.

Let cool slightly before serving. (The rhubarb can be roasted, cooled, and refrigerated for up to 2 days. Reheat gently before using, without stirring, in a microwave oven or in a covered dish in the oven.)

Spoon the warm rhubarb into 4 shallow dessert bowls. Place a small scoop (about ¼ cup) of the ice cream in the center, where it will begin to melt. Serve immediately.

1 orange

1 pound fresh or frozen rhubarb stalks, thawed, sliced about ½ inch thick

½ cup granulated sugar

2 tablespoons chopped candied ginger

1 cup vanilla ice cream

RHUBARB COBBLER

6 SERVINGS

RHUBARB COBBLER IS ONE OF my culinary benchmarks for springtime. Early in the season, when there is still a chill in the air, I love it plain, warm from the oven. By the end of May, when the weather is finally predictably warm, it seems right to top the cobbler with vanilla ice cream. Because rhubarb is one of the few fruits that freezes well, you can even have springtime in February if you like.

1½ pounds fresh or frozen rhubarb stalks, thawed, cut into 1-inch chunks

1 cup granulated sugar

1 cup plus 1 tablespoon all-purpose flour

1 teaspoon baking powder

½ teaspoon baking soda

4 tablespoons (½ stick) unsalted butter, cut into small pieces

⅔ cup buttermilk

Preheat the oven to 425 degrees. Generously butter a 1½-to-2-quart shallow baking dish or a 10-inch pie plate. Place the rhubarb in the baking dish and sprinkle it with ¾ cup of the sugar and 1 tablespoon of the flour. Use a fork or your fingers to toss and mix the fruit, sugar, and flour, then spread it evenly. Bake for 10 minutes.

Meanwhile, in a food processor, combine 3 tablespoons of the sugar, the remaining 1 cup flour, the baking powder, and baking soda. Add the butter and pulse to make coarse crumbs. With the motor running, pour the buttermilk through the feed tube and process just until a soft dough forms, about 6 seconds.

Remove the fruit from the oven and drop the dough from a spoon on top of the hot fruit to make 6 mounds. Sprinkle the dough with the remaining 1 tablespoon sugar and bake until the fruit is bubbly and the topping is golden brown, about 20 minutes. Serve warm.

ROASTED STRAWBERRIES

4 SERVINGS

Preheat the oven to 450 degrees. In an ovenproof skillet just large enough to hold the strawberries in one layer, melt the butter in the oven, 2 to 3 minutes. Watch carefully so that it does not burn. Remove the skillet from the oven and stir in 2 tablespoons of the sugar; the mixture will be grainy. Add the berries, tossing to coat them. Spread in a single layer. Roast, stirring and turning once or twice, until the berries just begin to soften and the sugar melts, about 5 minutes. Gently roll the roasted berries in the pan syrup to coat, then let them cool for about 5 minutes in the skillet.

Meanwhile, whip the cream with the liqueur and the remaining 1 tablespoon granulated sugar just until soft peaks form. Divide the cream among 4 shallow dessert bowls. Arrange the lukewarm berries in the cream, pointed ends up. Using a teaspoon, dribble the pan syrup over the cream. Garnish with the mint sprigs, if desired. Serve immediately.

1 tablespoon unsalted butter

3 tablespoons granulated sugar

16 large, perfect strawberries, preferably with stems

1 cup heavy cream, chilled

2 tablespoons amaretto or orange liqueur, such as Grand Marnier or Cointreau

4 fresh mint sprigs (optional)

A FEW MINUTES OF SIMMERING makes most blueberries taste infinitely more "berryish," and the sweet-sour addition of a little honey-and-fruit vinegar forms a brilliant indigo sauce. The warm sauce can be ladled over snowy white angel food cake or pound cake. The warm berries are also delicious served in bowls with a scoop of vanilla ice cream in the center.

BLUEBERRY ANGEL

4 TO 6 SERVINGS

1 pint fresh blueberries

¼ cup blueberry or other fruit vinegar

¼ cup honey

¼ cup crème de cassis or black currant syrup

4-6 slices purchased angel food cake, toasted, if desired

In a medium nonreactive saucepan, bring the blueberries, vinegar, honey, and crème de cassis or syrup to a simmer, stirring over medium heat until the berries just begin to burst, 3 to 5 minutes. (The berries can be cooled and refrigerated for 1 day. Reheat gently before serving.)

Spoon the warm berries and sauce over the angel food cake slices on dessert plates.

BROILED PEACH CRUNCH

4 SERVINGS

EVEN QUICKER AND EASIER than a cobbler or crumble, this quickly broiled peach dessert combines fresh, juicy fruit with a crunchy, buttery topping. I like it with a little heavy cream on top.

Drop the peaches into a pan of boiling water for about 15 seconds to loosen the skins. Use a small knife to slip off the skins. Pit and slice the peaches. In a 12- or 14-inch oval gratin dish or 9-inch pie plate, toss the peaches with the bourbon or nectar and lemon juice.

In a food processor, pulse the brown sugar, walnuts, and flour to combine. Add the butter and pulse until pea-sized crumbs form. Sprinkle the mixture over the peaches.

Broil about 6 inches from the heat source until the topping is crisp and browned, about 3 minutes. Serve family-style from the baking dish, or spoon onto 4 dessert plates.

1½ pounds ripe peaches

2 tablespoons bourbon or canned peach nectar

1 tablespoon lemon juice

6 tablespoons packed light brown sugar

¼ cup coarsely chopped walnuts

4 teaspoons all-purpose flour

4 tablespoons (½ stick) unsalted butter, chilled and cut into pieces

MANY FRUITS TAKE WELL TO roasting. Peaches are especially good this way because roasting loosens the skins, making a separate blanching step unnecessary. Toast the cake slices in the hot oven or, if you have time, make homemade drop biscuits, such as the shortcakes on page 180.

ROASTED PEACHES WITH POUND CAKE AND PISTACHIO ICE CREAM

4 SERVINGS

1 lemon

1 tablespoon unsalted butter

2 tablespoons packed light brown sugar

1 pound ripe peaches, pitted and thickly sliced

4 slices purchased pound cake, each about ¾ inch thick

1 pint pistachio or vanilla ice cream

Preheat the oven to 450 degrees. Grate 1 teaspoon of the colored part of the peel from the lemon and squeeze 2 teaspoons juice.

In a medium, ovenproof skillet, melt the butter with the brown sugar, stirring until blended. Add the peaches, lemon peel, and juice, stirring to coat the peaches. Place the skillet in the oven and roast, stirring gently once or twice, until the peaches are softened but maintain their shape, 5 to 10 minutes. At the same time, place the pound cake slices directly on the oven rack and toast until golden, 4 to 5 minutes. Leave the oven on.

Remove the skillet and the pound cake from the oven. Let the peaches cool in the syrup just enough so they can be handled. Remove their skins. Return the peaches to the oven and warm for about 2 minutes.

Place the pound cake slices on 4 dessert plates. Top with scoops of the ice cream. Spoon the warm peaches and sauce over and around the ice cream and pound cake. Serve immediately.

Grilled Pound Cake with Nectarines

4 SERVINGS

THE SIMPLE PROCESS OF toasting gives a rich caramelized edge to purchased pound cake. Here, the toasted slices are transformed into an elegant finale when they are layered with nectarine slices and brushed with a shiny, buttery jam glaze. Plums, peaches, apples, and pears take well to the same treatment.

Preheat the broiler. Grate 1 teaspoon of the colored part of the peel from the lemon and squeeze 1 tablespoon juice. In a small saucepan over medium-low heat, melt the preserves and butter. Stir in the lemon peel and juice.

Place the pound cake slices on a small baking sheet and set under the broiler about 4 inches from the heat source. Broil until golden brown, 1 to 2 minutes. Turn and brush lightly with some of the jam mixture. Arrange the nectarine slices, slightly overlapping, on the pound cake, then brush with the remaining jam mixture. Broil until the jam mixture is bubbly, about 1 minute.

Transfer the cake to 4 dessert plates. Sprinkle with the chopped mint and serve immediately, garnished with the mint sprigs.

1 lemon

¼ cup peach preserves

1 tablespoon unsalted butter

4 slices purchased pound cake, each about ¾ inch thick

2 nectarines, sliced

¼ cup chopped mint, plus 4 sprigs for garnish

APRICOTS POACHED IN SAUTERNES

4 SERVINGS

1 orange

1 cup Sauternes or muscatel wine

¼ cup granulated sugar

8 cardamom pods, lightly crushed

1½ pounds fresh apricots (about 8), pitted and halved or quartered

2 teaspoons rose water

Use a small knife to cut 3 long strips from the colored part of the orange peel. Squeeze ¼ cup juice.

In a medium nonreactive saucepan, combine the wine, sugar, cardamom pods, orange peel, and juice. Bring to a boil over high heat, stirring to dissolve the sugar. Add the apricots to the syrup, reduce the heat to medium-low, cover the pan, and simmer until the apricots are just fork-tender, about 5 minutes. Use a slotted spoon to transfer the apricots to a bowl, slip off and discard the skins, then place the fruit in the refrigerator.

Boil the poaching syrup over high heat until it is reduced to about 1 cup, about 5 minutes. Stir in the rose water. Pour the syrup over the apricots and let stand at least 10 minutes before serving warm, or refrigerate for up to 24 hours, then serve at a cool room temperature.

BROILED FRESH FIGS

2 SERVINGS

THINK OF THIS DESSERT WHEN you need a romantic late summer ending to a meal for two. It's simple, quick, warm, soft, and fragrant.

Preheat the broiler. Grate 1 teaspoon of the colored part of the peel from the lemon and squeeze 1½ tablespoons juice. Generously butter 2 gratin or other individual ovenproof baking dishes.

Arrange the figs, cut sides up, in a single layer in the buttered dishes. Sprinkle with the brown sugar, butter, and lemon peel. Dribble with the lemon juice.

Broil, about 4 inches from the heat source, until the sugar is melted and bubbly, 1 to 2 minutes. Watch carefully to prevent burning. Serve immediately.

1 lemon

4 fresh figs, stemmed and quartered

2 tablespoons packed light brown sugar

1 tablespoon unsalted butter, cut into 8 pieces

Most plums come to market underripe and tart, but cooking brings out the best in them, making them sweet and juicy. Any firm red, blue, or purple plum will work in this old-fashioned dessert, though I especially like Italian prune plums for their luscious texture. Plums are particularly convenient for baking because they need so little advance preparation: they require no peeling, and the pits separate from the fruit with ease. As with all crisps, this one is best served warm on the day of baking. It will taste just fine the next morning for breakfast but will need to be reheated in the oven to restore some of its crispness.

1 orange

1 pound firm plums, preferably Italian prune plums

8 tablespoons packed light brown sugar

½ cup quick oats

½ cup all-purpose flour

4 tablespoons (½ stick) unsalted butter, chilled and cut into 12 pieces

Plum Oatmeal Crisp

6 servings

Preheat the oven to 400 degrees. Generously butter a 9-inch pie plate or other similar-sized baking dish. Grate 1 teaspoon of the colored part of the peel from the orange and squeeze 2 tablespoons juice.

Pit and slice large plums (quarter prune plums). Place them in the pie plate along with 3 tablespoons of the brown sugar and the orange juice. Toss to mix, then spread evenly in the pie plate.

In a food processor, mix the oats, flour, remaining 5 tablespoons brown sugar, and orange peel. Distribute the butter over the mixture. Pulse to process into small clumps, about 10 seconds. Sprinkle the topping over the fruit to within 1 inch of the edge.

Bake until the topping is browned and crisp and the fruit is bubbly, about 25 minutes. Serve warm or at room temperature.

Plum Tostadas

4 SERVINGS

I LOVE THE RUSTIC FLAVOR OF corn tortillas with the rich sweetness of plums—the combination is similar to corn bread with jam. Here, sugared corn tortillas are baked until crisp and caramelized, then topped with warm sautéed plums. Any ripe, full-flavored variety of plum is good, though deep red or purple varieties are the prettiest.

Preheat the oven to 400 degrees. Grate 1 teaspoon of the colored part of the peel from the lemon and squeeze 1 tablespoon juice.

In a medium skillet, melt the butter. Place the tortillas on a baking sheet and brush a total of ½ tablespoon of the butter on one side of each. Sprinkle each side with a total of 1 tablespoon of the sugar. Place the tortillas in the oven to toast until they are crisp and the sugar begins to melt, 5 to 6 minutes.

Meanwhile, add the remaining 4 tablespoons sugar, lemon peel, and juice to the remaining 2 tablespoons butter in the skillet. Add the plums and cook over medium heat, stirring often, until they are softened, the sugar is melted, and a syrup forms, 5 to 10 minutes. Add the brandy or orange juice and cook for 2 minutes more.

Transfer the tortillas to 4 dessert plates, spoon the warm plum mixture onto each, and serve immediately.

1 lemon

2½ tablespoons unsalted butter

4 (8-inch) corn or flour tortillas

5 tablespoons granulated sugar

1 pound ripe plums, pitted and thickly sliced

3 tablespoons cognac, other brandy, or orange juice

BRAISED PLUMS WITH GINGER AND STAR ANISE

4 SERVINGS

THE FLAVOR OF PLUMS IS greatly enhanced by even a brief heating, but I find that the delicate flesh often dissolves into mush when the fruits are poached. Braising gently for just a few minutes in a highly aromatic liquid preserves the texture, while bringing out the best in the taste. Star anise is an exotic but easily obtainable spice that contributes a subtle licorice flavor.

2 lemons

6 star anise

8 dime-sized slices fresh ginger

4 tablespoons granulated sugar

1 pound (about 5) plums, red, green, black, or an assortment, thickly sliced

Use a small sharp knife or zester to peel 8 thin strips of the colored part of the peel from the lemon, then squeeze 2 tablespoons juice. In a medium skillet with a lid, bring the lemon peel and juice, anise, ginger, sugar, and ¼ cup water to a simmer, stirring to dissolve the sugar. Add the plums, spooning the liquid over. Cover the pan and simmer, stirring gently two or three times, until the plums are tender but not falling apart, about 5 minutes.

Transfer the plums and braising liquid directly from the skillet to 4 shallow dessert bowls. (Or chill the fruit in the liquid for up to 4 hours, returning to a cool room temperature before serving.)

ROASTED PEARS WITH AMARETTI CRUMBLE

4 SERVINGS

WARM FRUIT DESSERTS WITH crumbly nut toppings are as American as apple crisp, but Italians also appreciate them. In Italy, pears and almonds are often roasted or baked to intensify their flavors. This adaptation of an Italian classic is particularly quick and easy with crumbled amaretti as the crisp topping. I serve it at my traditional seafood Christmas Eve supper.

Preheat the oven to 400 degrees. Butter a shallow 2-quart baking or gratin dish. Grate 1 teaspoon of the colored part of the peel from the lemon and squeeze 1 tablespoon juice.

Peel, core, and thickly slice the pears. Place the pears in the dish and toss with the lemon peel and juice. Pour the sherry or marsala over and around the pears. Sprinkle with the butter pieces, then with the brown sugar, and finally with the crumbled amaretti. Bake, uncovered, basting the pears with the juices two or three times, until they are tender and the amaretti are browned, about 20 minutes.

Serve the pears warm with the juices spooned over them.

1 lemon

4 ripe but firm pears, such as Bosc or Anjou

⅓ cup dry sherry or marsala

2 tablespoons unsalted butter, cut into small pieces

2 tablespoons packed light brown sugar

½ cup crumbled amaretti cookies (about 4 double amaretti)

SECKEL PEARS ARE SMALL AND
very pretty, but if you can't find
them, substitute four of any other
small ripe, firm pears, peeled, cored,
and halved. During the holidays, you
can buy containers of mixed whole
spices, usually called "mulling
spices," which often include whole
cloves, allspice, a cinnamon stick,
and perhaps a cardamom pod. You
can use any combination of these or
other aromatic whole spices that you
have on hand. A spiced or flavored
tea will add yet another dimension to
the pears. I like to serve them with
the whole spices still in the poaching
liquid.

1 orange

8 Seckel pears (1-1½ pounds)

2 tea bags, such as Earl Grey or a
    spiced tea

1 cup orange muscatel, other sweet
    dessert wine, or white grape juice

⅓ cup granulated sugar

1 tablespoon mixed whole mulling
    spices

TEA-POACHED SECKEL PEARS

4 SERVINGS

Use a small sharp knife or zester to cut 3 strips of the colored part
of the orange peel. Squeeze ¼ cup juice. Peel the pears, but do not
core them. In a 2- or 3 -quart nonreactive saucepan, combine the tea
bags, wine or grape juice, sugar, spices, orange peel and juice, and 1
cup water. Add the pears. (If the liquid does not barely cover the
pears, add a bit more water.)

Bring the mixture to a simmer, cover, and cook for 5 minutes. Remove and discard the tea bags, turn the pears, then cover again and
simmer until they are just fork-tender, 5 to 10 minutes more. Use a
slotted spoon to remove the pears from the poaching syrup and refrigerate them to cool slightly.

Boil the syrup until it is reduced by about half, 5 to 10 minutes. Pour
the hot syrup over the cool pears, and let them stand for at least 10
minutes or refrigerate up to 6 hours. Reheat gently before serving.
Serve the pears warm with the poaching syrup spooned over them.

BOURBON BAKED APPLES

4 SERVINGS

Preheat the oven to 400 degrees. Butter a shallow 2-quart baking dish or other dish just large enough to hold 8 apple halves in a single layer. Grate 1 teaspoon of the colored part of the peel from the lemon and squeeze 1 tablespoon juice. Cut the apples in half, then core them.

Place the apple halves, cut side up, in the baking dish. Sprinkle with the lemon juice and bourbon or apple juice concentrate. Pour 2 tablespoons water around, not over, the apples. In a small dish, use your fingers to rub together the butter, brown sugar, pie spice, and lemon peel until crumbly. Sprinkle evenly over the cut sides of the apples.

Bake, spooning the juices over the apples once or twice, until the apples are just fork-tender, 20 to 25 minutes. Serve warm with the pan juices spooned over them.

1 lemon

4 small tart apples (about 1½ pounds)

8 teaspoons bourbon or frozen apple juice concentrate, thawed

2 tablespoons unsalted butter, chilled and cut into small pieces

⅓ cup packed dark brown sugar

½ teaspoon apple or pumpkin pie spice

SOUSED CINNAMON AND CIDER APPLES

4 SERVINGS

2 pounds tart apples, peeled, cored, and cut into rough ¾-inch chunks

½ cup packed light brown sugar

½ cup apple cider

½ cup apple brandy, such as Calvados or applejack, or additional cider

2 tablespoons unsalted butter

¾ teaspoon ground cinnamon

1 cup vanilla or butter-pecan ice cream

In a large heavy saucepan, combine the apples, brown sugar, cider, apple brandy or additional cider, butter, and cinnamon. Cover and cook over medium-low heat, stirring occasionally, until the apples are very tender, 10 to 15 minutes. Uncover and simmer until the liquid is lightly reduced, about 10 minutes. Use the back of a wooden spoon to mash some of the apples, while leaving others chunky. (The apples can be refrigerated for up to 3 days. Reheat before serving.)

To serve, divide the warm apples among 4 dessert dishes. Top each serving with a small scoop of ice cream.

CRANBERRY-RASPBERRY COMPOTE

6 SERVINGS

THIS LIGHT AND MARVELOUSLY easy addition to a Thanksgiving dessert array can be served warm or at room temperature, spooned over angel food or pound cake slices, vanilla ice cream, or over a large sugar cookie as a cranberry "tart."

In a medium nonreactive saucepan, combine the cranberries and sugar. Cook over medium heat, stirring almost constantly, until the cranberries have popped, the sugar dissolves, and a thick sauce forms, about 5 minutes. Cook and stir 1 minute longer. Remove from the heat and stir in the jam and liqueur or syrup. Cool about 10 minutes until lukewarm. (The compote can be refrigerated for up to 5 days, or frozen for up to 1 month. Warm gently before using.)

To serve, arrange the cookies on individual dessert plates. Spoon the warm compote over the cookies.

1 12-ounce bag (about 3 cups) fresh cranberries

½ cup granulated sugar

1 cup seedless raspberry jam

3 tablespoons raspberry liqueur, such as Framboise, or cognac, or raspberry syrup

6 large (at least 3 inches in diameter) crisp sugar cookies

CRANBERRY-APPLE BURRITOS

4 SERVINGS

¼ cup granulated sugar

1¼ teaspoons ground cinnamon

2 tablespoons unsalted butter

2 tart apples, peeled, cored, and thinly sliced

¼ cup dried cranberries

3 tablespoons apple brandy, such as Calvados or applejack, or cider

4 (8-inch) flour tortillas

½ cup vanilla yogurt or frozen yogurt (optional)

In a small dish, combine the sugar and cinnamon. In a medium skillet, heat the butter and cook the apples, stirring often, over medium heat for 2 minutes, or until they begin to soften. Add the cranberries and all but 2 teaspoons of the cinnamon sugar. Continue to cook, stirring, until the sugar melts and caramelizes and the apples are tender, 3 to 5 minutes. Stir in the brandy or cider and cook 2 minutes more.

Warm the tortillas in a microwave for a few seconds wrapped in plastic. Or preheat the oven to 350 degrees, wrap in foil, and warm for about 5 minutes. Transfer the tortillas to 4 dessert plates.

To serve, spoon the filling down the center of each tortilla. Fold the bottom edge of the tortillas up over the filling. Fold in the sides. Roll up to enclose the filling. Sprinkle the tops with the remaining cinnamon sugar. Serve immediately with a dollop of yogurt or with a scoop of frozen yogurt, if desired.

MAPLE-GRILLED POLENTA AND APPLES

6 SERVINGS

Prepare a medium barbecue fire or preheat the broiler. Grate 1 teaspoon of the colored part of the peel from the lemon and squeeze 2 tablespoons juice.

In a small saucepan, heat together the maple syrup, butter, cinnamon, lemon peel, and juice until the mixture is bubbly and the butter melts. Simmer the sauce over medium-low heat until slightly reduced, about 5 minutes.

Meanwhile, cut the polenta crosswise into 12 slices. Core the unpeeled apples and cut each one crosswise into 6 slices. Brush both sides of the apple and polenta slices with some of the maple sauce. Grill, turning once or twice and brushing with more sauce, until the polenta is golden and lightly charred and the apples are just tender, about 8 minutes total for the polenta and about 6 minutes for the apples. Transfer 2 polenta slices to each of 6 dessert plates.

To serve, place an apple slice on top of each polenta slice. Drizzle or brush with any remaining maple mixture.

POLENTA HAS MYRIAD USES IN savory recipes, but it is also an ingredient in Tuscan desserts, one of which inspired this autumnal favorite of mine. Prepared polenta rolls are found in the refrigerated or deli section of the market. The oven broiler does a fine job with this dessert if you don't have the grill fired up.

1 large lemon

½ cup maple syrup

2 tablespoons unsalted butter

¾ teaspoon ground cinnamon

1 roll (about 1 pound) prepared plain polenta

2 tart medium-sized apples

Peanut Butter Panini with Concord Grapes

4 SERVINGS

My Sicilian grandparents were Concord grape growers in western New York State along the Lake Erie shore, and we enjoyed grapes in every imaginable form. These sweet "sandwiches" of pound cake spread with peanut butter and fresh grape preserves are a sweet twist on my favorite childhood sandwich. Concord grapes have a short season, so make this dessert in early fall during the harvest.

2 cups Concord grapes, plus 4 small clusters for garnish

½ cup granulated sugar

1 tablespoon lemon juice

8 slices purchased pound cake, each about ½ inch thick

¼ cup smooth or chunky, regular or reduced-fat peanut butter, at room temperature

¼ cup coarsely chopped unsalted peanuts

In a medium skillet or saucepan, cook the 2 cups grapes with the sugar and lemon juice over medium heat, mashing often, until the grapes have separated from the skins and the pulp has dissolved into a bubbly, deep purple sauce, 5 to 7 minutes. Strain the sauce, mashing hard on the skins to extract all of the grape puree. (The sauce can be prepared a day ahead and refrigerated. Reheat gently before serving.)

Toast both sides of the pound cake slices in a toaster or on a baking sheet set under the broiler. Spread one side of the hot cake slices with peanut butter, then arrange them on 4 dessert plates. Spoon the warm grape sauce over the cake, sprinkle with the peanuts, and garnish the plates with the grape clusters. Serve immediately.

Calypso Kabobs

4 SERVINGS

If using bamboo skewers, soak 8 of them in water for at least 15 minutes. Prepare a medium barbecue fire or preheat the broiler. Grate 1 teaspoon of the colored part of the peel from the lime and squeeze 2 tablespoons juice.

In a small saucepan, heat the honey, butter, lime peel, and juice, stirring just until the butter melts.

Peel and remove the seed from the mango; peel and seed the papaya. Cut each into 8 chunks. Peel the banana and cut crosswise into 8 slices. Thread 1 piece each of the fruits on each of the skewers. Brush with some of the honey mixture.

Grill the kabobs or place on a small baking sheet and broil, turning once carefully and brushing again, just until softened and lightly touched with gold, 2 to 4 minutes. Arrange the kabobs on 4 dessert plates and drizzle or brush with the remaining honey sauce. Serve immediately.

TROPICAL FRUITS SEEM TO take especially well to gentle heating over the embers of the backyard barbecue. This light dessert is well suited to finish off a sturdy slab of ribs or a big smoky brisket, and off-season, you can use your oven broiler to conjure up the taste of summer and top off a winter meal. Bamboo skewers make the prettiest presentation. Soak them in water for at least 15 minutes before grilling, or they will become kindling for the fire. You can use small metal skewers, but warn diners that they are hot.

1 large or 2 small limes

¼ cup honey

1 tablespoon unsalted butter

1 mango

1 papaya

1 large, firm banana

⅔ cup heavy cream

12 ounces chopped bittersweet chocolate or 2 cups semisweet chocolate chips

1 cinnamon stick, broken in half, or ½ teaspoon ground cinnamon

1 vanilla bean, split lengthwise, or 1 teaspoon vanilla extract

8 cups chunked or sliced tropical fruits, such as bananas, mangoes, papayas, pineapples, or seedless orange or tangerine sections

MEXICAN CHOCOLATE AND TROPICAL FRUIT FONDUE

6 SERVINGS

Place the cream, chocolate, and cinnamon in a medium bowl (ceramic or glass, if you plan to use your microwave for the next step). Scrape the seeds from the vanilla bean into the cream mixture, then add the bean (reserve the vanilla extract, if using). Set the bowl over a pan of simmering water or in a microwave oven, and heat, stirring once or twice, until the chocolate is nearly melted. Remove from the heat and stir until smooth; stir in the vanilla extract, if using. (The fondue can be cooled and refrigerated for up to 3 days, with or without the cinnamon stick and vanilla bean, depending upon how strong you like the flavor. Reheat the fondue gently before using.)

Serve the fondue in a fondue pot or in a small deep pot set over another pot of hot water to keep it warm. Surround the fondue with the fruit, and use long toothpicks, bamboo skewers, or fondue forks for dipping.

MANGO-BANANA GRATIN

4 SERVINGS

Preheat the broiler. Lightly brush 4 broiler-proof gratin dishes or 1 broiler-proof platter with about ½ tablespoon of the butter. Arrange the banana and mango slices, overlapping, on each gratin dish. Drizzle with the lime juice. In a small bowl, stir together the brown sugar and allspice. Sprinkle evenly over the fruit. Drizzle with the remaining 1½ tablespoons butter.

Broil until the sugar is melted and bubbly and the fruit is golden, about 2 minutes. Sprinkle with the coconut and broil until lightly toasted, about 30 seconds more. Serve immediately.

BROILING IS THE QUICKEST way to cook fruit, and the fast, intense heat also caramelizes the fruit's exterior. When choosing a mango, look for one that is unblemished and yields slightly to pressure. Bananas are at their best when they are completely yellow, with just a few brownish spots beginning to appear. After that, they become very sweet, but too mushy to remain firm during broiling. Other tropical fruits, such as papayas or pineapple, also taste wonderful prepared in this manner.

2 tablespoons unsalted butter, melted

2 large, firm bananas, peeled and sliced

1 large mango, peeled, seeded, and sliced about ¼ inch thick

2 tablespoons lime juice

¼ cup packed light brown sugar

¾ teaspoon ground allspice

¼ cup sweetened shredded coconut

ROASTED SESAME BANANAS

4 SERVINGS

BECAUSE THIS IS A QUICK baked version of the classic fried banana dessert found on many Chinese menus, I often serve it after a stir-fry. It also makes a fine late-night snack or early-morning breakfast.

1 orange

1½ tablespoons unsalted butter

1 tablespoon honey

4 small, very firm, slightly underripe bananas, peeled

3 tablespoons sesame seeds

Preheat the oven to 500 degrees. Grate 2 teaspoons of the colored part of the peel from the orange and squeeze 1 tablespoon juice. In a small skillet, melt the butter with the honey, orange peel, and juice.

Roll the bananas in the butter mixture, then sprinkle evenly on all sides with the sesame seeds. (Reserve any remaining sauce.) Place on a small baking sheet. Bake, without turning, until the seeds and orange peel are lightly charred and the bananas are slightly softened, 8 to 10 minutes. Transfer the bananas to 4 dessert plates. Serve the bananas immediately, drizzled with any remaining butter sauce.

FROZEN DESSERTS

ICE CREAM WAS MY FATHER'S VICE, AND HE MADE IT MINE, TOO. MY EARLIEST memory is of the Good Humor man coming up our block ringing his bell, while my sister and brother and I waited with a nickel clenched in our fists. From the day it opened, my dad was probably the Dairy Queen's premier customer, and he took us there for any celebration, from winning a Little League game to losing a tooth.

The habit carries over to my adulthood. When electric ice-cream makers were all the rage, I immediately bought one, but it took up too much counter space. Fortunately, at about the same time, Ben, Jerry, and several other talented entrepreneurs began making ice cream that was as good as homemade. I donated my ice-cream machine to a garage sale.

Ice cream now takes up more room in the supermarket freezer than vegetables, and there are types for every taste, health persuasion, and pocketbook. Ice cream with the fewest ingredients is far more like homemade and is almost always of good quality. For vanilla, my own (and America's) favorite, buy brands made with pure extract or vanilla beans. Chocolate ice cream should contain real chocolate or cocoa. Coffee ice cream should be made from real coffee beans.

With the rainbow repertoire of sauces and toppings that follow—and a few good ice creams in your freezer—you can stock an enviable home ice-cream parlor, where the treats are ready in less time than it takes to drive to the local sweet shop and far more tempting.

DESSERT MARGARITAS

4 SERVINGS

TAKING ITS CUE FROM THE famous cocktail, this dessert margarita has a light, refreshing, puckery sweetness that produces just the right finish after a spicy Mexican supper. If you don't have classic margarita glasses, use martini or wide-edged wine goblets. Dark chocolate wafer cookies make a perfect Mexican-style accompaniment. You can serve the syrup over passion fruit or mango sorbet as well.

4-5 fresh unblemished green-skinned limes

5 tablespoons granulated sugar

3 tablespoons tequila

3 tablespoons Triple Sec

1 pint lime sorbet

Cut 4 thin crosswise slices from the center of 1 of the limes and set them aside for the garnish. Use a small sharp knife or zester to cut the colored part of the peel from the remaining limes. Cut the peel into thin strips (about ⅛ inch thick); you should have about ¼ cup. Place in a small saucepan and add enough water to cover by 1 inch. Cover and simmer the lime peels over medium heat for 3 minutes; drain and discard the water.

Add 3 tablespoons of the sugar and 3 tablespoons water to the peel. Cook, stirring, until the sugar is dissolved, about 2 minutes. Bring to a boil, stirring, over medium-high heat; cover and simmer for 1 minute. Uncover and simmer for 1 minute. Transfer the peel and syrup to a small dish; let cool. Stir in the tequila and Triple Sec. (The syrup and peel can be refrigerated for up to 2 days; return to room temperature before using.)

Just before serving, moisten the rims of 4 margarita glasses with water. Place the remaining 2 tablespoons sugar on a saucer, then dip the glasses into the sugar to coat. Scoop the sorbet into the glasses, drizzle each with 2 tablespoons of the syrup and garnish with the lime slices.

Flash-Frozen Quickies

Here are some great ideas for fabulous frozen desserts that are so quick and easy that you don't even need a recipe.

Iced Champagne Grapes: Place small clusters of champagne grapes (or other varieties) on a small tray in the freezer for at least 30 minutes or up to 6 hours. Serve with a plate of buttery cookies or use as a garnish to keep glasses of champagne chilled.

Ice Cream Cone Creations: Set out several flavors of ice cream and some sugar cones. Have ready shallow dishes of miniature chocolate chips, chopped toasted nuts, toasted coconut, crushed malted milk balls, chopped candied ginger, crushed toffee candy bars, and/or chopped dried mixed fruit tidbits. Have each guest assemble an ice cream cone and then roll it in a topping. You can decide whether double-dipping is allowed!

Herb or Spice Sprinkles: Sprinkle scoops of ice cream or sorbet with chopped fresh herbs, such as sage, basil, or mint, or a dusting of dried spices, such as cinnamon, nutmeg, cloves, or cardamom. Serve the herbed ice cream garnished with a sprig of herbs and the spiced iced cream with an edible, organic flower blossom, such as a nasturtium or marigold.

CITRUS BOWLS: Cut off the tops of lemons, oranges, or limes, then use a grapefruit spoon to scoop out all of the fruit. Reserve the fruit pulp for other uses. Pat the inside of the fruit shells dry with paper toweling. Fill the shells to overflowing with melon ball-sized scoops of assorted colors of sorbets. Serve immediately or freeze for up to 6 hours before serving. If desired, drizzle the sorbet balls with a bit of liqueur just before serving. Replace the top fruit slice as a top hat and garnish with a mint sprig, if desired.

EASIEST-EVER FRUIT SORBET

3 SERVINGS

RIGHT UP FRONT YOU NEED TO know that this recipe takes longer to prepare than any other in this book. You also need to know that it is the easiest and most versatile. Here it is in a nutshell (or a can). Put a can of fruit in the freezer for at least 12 hours. When it is frozen, open the can and put the contents in a food processor. Add a little lemon juice and puree. Stop snickering. This just might be the best recipe you'll ever make. Try it once and your freezer will never again be without a can of fruit at the ready. Here are the proportions and some delicious variations on the theme. My own favorites are apricot and fig.

1 can (15-to-17 ounces) fruit in heavy (not light) syrup

2 teaspoons lemon juice

1 tablespoon liqueur (optional)

Place the unopened can in the freezer for at least 12 hours, or until frozen solid. (The fruit can be left frozen for several months.) Submerge the unopened can in hot water for a few seconds to loosen the edges, then open the can and transfer the contents to a food processor, using a kitchen knife to cut it into several chunks. Add the lemon juice and liqueur, if using.

Process, pulsing on and off until smooth, 10 to 15 seconds. Scoop the sorbet into balls and serve immediately or refreeze for up to 8 hours before serving.

Be sure to use fruit in heavy syrup.

- sliced or halved apricots with amaretto

- figs with marsala or Sambuca

- sliced or halved pears with Poire William or green crème de mènthe

- sliced or halved peaches with bourbon

- plums (remove pits) with crème de cassis

- crushed pineapple with dark rum (and 2 tablespoons canned cream of coconut for a piña colada)

- blueberries with crème de cassis

- sweet cherries with kirsch

- mangoes with light rum

- litchi nuts with dark rum

SCOTCH BUTTERSCOTCH SAUCE

MAKES ABOUT I CUP

WITH BOTH BUTTER AND Scotch, this sauce is the real thing! It's infinitely better than the kind you buy in a jar, and it takes only about 10 minutes to make. Serve it over ice cream or over grilled pineapple slices or with both together, or as a dessert waffle topping, along with sliced bananas and chopped walnuts.

1 cup packed light brown sugar

⅓ cup heavy cream

3 tablespoons unsalted butter

2 tablespoons dark corn syrup

2 tablespoons Scotch whisky

1 teaspoon vanilla extract

In a medium saucepan, slowly bring the brown sugar, cream, butter, and corn syrup to a boil over medium heat, stirring constantly to dissolve the sugar. Boil gently, stirring often, until the sauce thickens and coats the back of a spoon, 4 to 5 minutes. Remove from the heat and stir in the Scotch and vanilla until blended.

Let cool slightly before using. (The sauce can be refrigerated for up to 1 week. Warm gently before serving.)

Hot Fudge Sauce

MAKES ABOUT 1½ CUPS SAUCE,
ENOUGH FOR 6 SUNDAES

In a medium saucepan over medium-low heat, stir the chocolate, corn syrup, and espresso or coffee powder until the chocolate is melted and smooth. Stir in the cream and heat just to a simmer, stirring constantly. Remove from the heat and stir in the vanilla.

Let cool slightly before using. (The sauce can be refrigerated for up to 1 week. Warm gently before serving.)

HOT FUDGE IS THE MOST requested sundae in America. This simple sauce has all the right characteristics: it's warm, shiny, and sticks nicely to the ice cream as it rolls down the scoops in neat rivulets. Though chocolate is the pivotal ingredient, corn syrup is essential for the proper syrupy texture, and a touch of coffee intensifies the flavor.

Purists would never ladle this sauce over anything but vanilla ice cream, but I like coffee, peppermint stick, raspberry swirl, butter-pecan, or orange custard. You can add a sprinkling of nuts, a dollop of whipped cream, or a maraschino cherry.

6 ounces bittersweet chocolate, chopped, or 1 cup semisweet chocolate chips

½ cup light corn syrup

2 teaspoons instant espresso or coffee powder

¼ cup heavy cream

1 teaspoon vanilla extract

REALLY LITTLE MORE THAN chocolate and cream melted together, this is the world's easiest chocolate sauce. Because of its simplicity, splurge on really good chocolate. Depending upon the temperature and proportion of chocolate to cream, ganache can also be made into truffles (page 223) and cake fillings or frostings. As a sauce, it should be slightly warmed until pourable. Serve it with ice cream, plain cakes, or fruit.

6 ounces (1 cup) semisweet chocolate chips or semisweet chocolate, chopped, either plain or flavored, such as mint, raspberry, almond, or coffee

½ cup heavy cream

½ teaspoon vanilla extract

1 tablespoon liqueur, such as Grand Marnier, amaretto, or Sambuca (optional)

CHOCOLATE GANACHE SAUCE

MAKES ABOUT 1 CUP

In a small saucepan over medium-low heat, stir the chocolate and cream until the chocolate is melted. Remove from the heat and stir until smooth. Stir in the vanilla and liqueur, if desired. (The sauce can be refrigerated, covered, for up to 1 week or frozen for up to 1 month.) Warm gently before serving.

CARAMEL APPLE FLAMBÉ

4 SERVINGS

CARAMEL APPLES ARE AMONG my nicest childhood memories—reminiscent of when Halloween was a carefree run through the neighborhood and the treats were almost always homemade. A fitting finale to an adult Halloween party, this dessert is also an affectionate nod to days gone by.

Toast the walnuts in a dry skillet over medium heat, stirring, until they are golden brown and fragrant, 2 to 4 minutes. Immediately remove them from the skillet to prevent burning. (Or toast on a small baking sheet in a 375-degree oven, stirring occasionally, for 5 to 8 minutes.)

Heat the butter in a medium skillet and cook the apples over medium heat, stirring often, just until they begin to soften and color, about 2 minutes. Sprinkle with the brown sugar and cinnamon. Continue to cook, stirring often, until the sugar caramelizes and the apples soften, 4 to 5 minutes. Remove the pan from the heat, add the brandy, and carefully ignite. Allow the flames to burn down.

Divide the ice cream among 4 shallow dessert bowls. Ladle the warm apples and sauce over the ice cream. Sprinkle with the nuts. Serve immediately.

⅓ cup coarsely chopped walnuts

2 tablespoons unsalted butter

2 large tart apples, peeled, cored, and thinly sliced

3 tablespoons packed light brown sugar

½ teaspoon ground cinnamon

2 tablespoons apple brandy, such as Calvados or applejack, or other brandy

1 pint vanilla or lemon custard ice cream or gelato

STRAWBERRIES AND RHUBARB share honors as two of the most important spring fruits and, as such, are classic pie fillings. But the same duet plays just as well as a topping for ice cream. The timing from start to finish is about 20 minutes . . . nearly as long as the oven takes to preheat for pie baking! This sweet-tart sauce makes a superb topping for dessert waffles and, when chilled, it's firm enough to stand in for jam on morning toast.

¾ pound fresh or frozen rhubarb, thawed, trimmed and cut into ½-inch slices

⅓ cup granulated sugar

⅓ cup orange juice

1 pint strawberries, hulled and sliced

2 tablespoons orange liqueur, such as Grand Marnier or Cointreau, or frozen orange juice concentrate, thawed

1 pint vanilla ice cream

STRAWBERRY-RHUBARB SUNDAES

4 SERVINGS

In a medium saucepan, bring the rhubarb, sugar, and orange juice to a simmer, stirring to dissolve the sugar. Cover the pan and simmer over medium heat, stirring occasionally, until the rhubarb is just soft, about 5 minutes. Stir in half of the strawberries and simmer for 2 minutes longer.

Remove from the heat and stir in the liqueur or orange juice concentrate. Let cool until tepid, about 10 minutes. (The sauce can be refrigerated at this point for up to 2 days. Rewarm gently before proceeding.) Stir in the remaining strawberries. Divide the ice cream among 4 dessert bowls and ladle the sauce over the ice cream. Serve immediately.

PUREED PEACHES AND FRESH RASPBERRY COUPE

4 SERVINGS

Dip the peaches into a pan of boiling water for about 15 seconds to loosen the skins. Use a small knife to slip off the skins. Pit the peaches and cut them into chunks. In a food processor, puree the peaches, liqueur or nectar, sugar, and vinegar. Let stand at room temperature for 10 minutes or refrigerate for up to 2 hours, removing from the refrigerator about 15 minutes before serving.

Divide the peach puree among 4 dessert dishes. Top with scoops of the ice cream. Sprinkle with the raspberries. Serve immediately.

IN THE CLASSIC COMBINATION of raspberries and peaches, it's the raspberries that are most often pureed. But because I love the shape of perfect fresh raspberries, I prefer to puree the peaches instead. Raspberry vinegar heightens the flavor of peaches that are not quite tree-ripe, as is so often the case with those that are sold in the supermarket. This showy dessert belies its 15-minute preparation.

1 pound ripe peaches

3 tablespoons peach schnapps, peach brandy, or canned peach nectar

2 tablespoons granulated sugar

2 teaspoons raspberry vinegar

1 pint vanilla ice cream

1 cup fresh raspberries

2 tablespoons unsalted butter

3 tablespoons packed light brown
   sugar

3 apricots, pitted and thickly sliced

1 tablespoon cognac, other brandy, or
   canned apricot nectar

1 tablespoon balsamic vinegar

1 cup pitted fresh sweet cherries

1 pint premium vanilla ice cream

APRICOT AND BALSAMIC CHERRY SUNDAES

4 SERVINGS

In a medium skillet, heat the butter and brown sugar, stirring, to melt the sugar. Add the apricots and cook, stirring gently, until just softened, about 3 minutes. Add the brandy or nectar, vinegar, and cherries. Simmer 2 minutes more.

Divide the ice cream among 4 dessert bowls. Spoon the warm fruit and sauce over the ice cream. Serve immediately.

Mango and Macaroon Sundaes

4 SERVINGS

TROPICAL MANGOES ARE A natural with coconut macaroons and island rum. It's a lot easier to dice a mango than to make neat slices because the fruit is very stubborn about separating from its pit. Diced is as good as sliced, so take the easy way out. Pineapples, peaches, apricots, or even pears also work well in this boozy, adult dessert.

Preheat the oven to 350 degrees. Spread the crumbled macaroons on a baking sheet and toast, stirring occasionally, until dark golden and fragrant, about 8 minutes. Cool slightly. (The macaroons can be toasted a day ahead and stored, tightly covered. Reheat slightly in a warm oven before using.)

In a medium bowl, combine the mangoes, sugar, rum, and lime juice. Let stand at room temperature, stirring occasionally, until the sugar dissolves and a syrup forms, 10 to 15 minutes.

Divide the ice cream among 4 dessert bowls. Spoon the fruit and syrup over, and sprinkle with the warm macaroon crumbs. Serve immediately.

1 cup crumbled coconut macaroons

2 mangoes, peeled and diced

3 tablespoons granulated sugar

¼ cup dark rum

1 tablespoon lime juice

1 pint vanilla ice cream

BLACKBERRY HONEYPOT SUNDAES

4 SERVINGS

THE BLACKBERRY IS OFTEN considered to be a poor relation to the esteemed raspberry. Its seediness does pose a problem, but when pureed and strained, it has a deep flavor that is unsurpassed. Slightly tangy lemon custard ice cream or frozen yogurt is the ideal base for these sundaes, but vanilla ice cream is always in good taste.

2 cups blackberries, fresh or frozen, thawed

2 tablespoons blackberry brandy or raspberry syrup

2 tablespoons orange juice

2 tablespoons berry-blossom honey

1 pint lemon custard ice cream, gelato, or frozen yogurt

1 cup fresh red or golden raspberries (optional)

In a food processor, puree the berries with the brandy or syrup, orange juice, and honey. Strain through a sieve into a small bowl, pushing hard on the seeds and solids. (The sauce can be refrigerated for up to 1 day. Return to room temperature before serving.)

Spoon the sauce into 4 dessert bowls. Scoop the ice cream or frozen yogurt over the sauce. Sprinkle with the raspberries, if desired. Serve immediately.

Key West Sunsets

4 SERVINGS

Grate 2 teaspoons of the colored part of the peel from the limes and squeeze 2 tablespoons juice. Grate 1 tablespoon of the colored part of the peel from the oranges, peel and thinly slice 1 orange, then squeeze ⅔ cup juice from the remaining 2 oranges.

In a medium skillet, combine the brown sugar, cardamom, lime and orange peels, and juices. Bring to a boil over medium heat, stirring constantly to dissolve the sugar. Simmer until slightly thickened, about 3 minutes. Add the orange and papaya slices and simmer for 2 minutes. Remove the pan from heat and immediately pour in the rum. Carefully ignite the sauce.

When the flames begin to die down, use a slotted spoon to remove the fruit and arrange on 4 dessert plates. Top the fruit with scoops of the ice cream. Spoon the hot sauce over the fruit and ice cream. Serve immediately.

THIS FIRE-AND-ICE DESSERT is nothing more than a brief sauté of sliced tropical fruit ignited and ladled over ice cream. In winter, the flaming fruit conjures the fantasy of a tropical vacation, and in the summer (the height of lime season), the dessert cools the palate after a spicy barbecue. If you are in the Florida Keys, bring home some fragrant native Key limes. Or make the dessert with ordinary limes, but be sure to look for heavy fruit with shiny dark green skins, indicating juiciness and freshness.

4 Key limes or 2 ordinary limes

3 oranges

½ cup packed light brown sugar

1 teaspoon ground cardamom

1 large papaya, peeled, seeded, and sliced

3 tablespoons dark rum

1 pint banana, mango, or vanilla ice cream

CANDIED GINGER AND BRANDIED PLUM SUNDAES

4 SERVINGS

1½ tablespoons unsalted butter

3 tablespoons granulated sugar

1 pound tart red or purple plums, such as Santa Rosas, thickly sliced

3 tablespoons brandy

3 tablespoons chopped candied ginger

1 pint vanilla, orange, or lemon custard ice cream, or gelato

In a medium skillet over medium heat, melt the butter with the sugar, stirring until bubbly and smooth. Add the plums and brandy, reduce the heat to medium-low, and simmer, uncovered, stirring often, until the plums are soft but not mushy, and the juices form a light syrup, about 5 minutes. Stir in the ginger and simmer for 30 seconds. Let cool slightly.

Divide the ice cream among 4 shallow dessert bowls or goblets. Spoon the warm plums and sauce over the ice cream. Serve immediately.

THE BIG EASY BUTTER-PECAN BANANAS FOSTER

4 SERVINGS

Grate 1½ teaspoons of the colored part of the peel from the lemon and squeeze 1½ tablespoons juice. Peel the bananas and cut in half lengthwise, then cut again in half crosswise.

In a medium skillet, heat the butter and brown sugar, stirring to melt the sugar. Add the bananas and lemon peel. Cook, stirring gently, over medium-low heat until the bananas are just softened, about 3 minutes. Stir in the lemon juice, then drizzle with the liqueur. Remove the skillet from the heat and carefully ignite the liqueur.

Divide the ice cream among 4 dessert bowls. Spoon the bananas and sauce over the ice cream. Serve immediately.

BANANAS FOSTER, THE decadent dessert of buttery sautéed bananas splashed with liqueur and ladled, flaming, over ice cream, was invented at Brennan's Restaurant in New Orleans and is synonymous with dining in the Big Easy. Equally famous are the pecan pralines that are sold all over the city. This streamlined version of Bananas Foster suggests pralines with butter-pecan ice cream. It is quick, easy, and just as decadent.

1 large lemon

4 small, firm bananas

2 tablespoons unsalted butter

¼ cup packed dark brown sugar

4 tablespoons B&B liqueur or brandy

1 pint butter-pecan ice cream

MAUI MADNESS

4 SERVINGS

⅓ cup coarsely chopped macadamia nuts

2 tablespoons unsalted butter

4 slices fresh pineapple

¼ cup molasses

2 tablespoons dark rum

1 tablespoon lemon juice

1 pint coffee ice cream

Lightly toast the nuts in a small dry skillet over medium heat, stirring, until they are golden and fragrant, about 2 minutes. Immediately remove from the skillet to prevent burning. (Or toast on a small baking sheet in a 375-degree oven, stirring occasionally, for 5 to 8 minutes.)

Melt the butter in a medium skillet and cook the pineapple over medium heat, turning once, until tinged with gold, about 2 minutes per side. Stir in the molasses and simmer, spooning the sauce over the fruit, for 3 minutes. Transfer the pineapple to 4 shallow dessert bowls. Add the rum and lemon juice to the skillet and simmer, stirring, until slightly thickened, about 2 minutes.

Place a scoop of the ice cream on each pineapple slice. Spoon the sauce over the ice cream. Sprinkle with the nuts and serve immediately.

CRANBERRY-ORANGE SUNDAES

4 SERVINGS

ANY WHOLE-BERRY CRANBERRY sauce will work in this inventive recipe. This sundae is so good that I cook up a batch of cranberry sauce just to make it.

In a heavy saucepan, combine the cranberry sauce, ¼ cup of the liqueur or orange juice, and orange peel. Stir over medium heat just until simmering. Let cool slightly. Stir in the remaining liqueur if the sauce seems too thick to ladle over the ice cream. (The sauce can be made up to 2 days ahead and refrigerated. Reheat before assembling the sundaes.)

Divide the ice cream among 4 dessert bowls. Ladle the warm sauce over each scoop. Serve immediately.

1¼ cups whole-berry cranberry sauce, preferably homemade

¼-⅓ cup cranberry or orange liqueur, such as Grand Marnier or Cointreau, or orange juice

2 teaspoons grated orange peel

1 pint vanilla ice cream

ICE CREAM WITH FLAMBÉED PRUNES AND ARMAGNAC

4 SERVINGS

⅓ cup granulated sugar

⅔ cup orange juice

6 ounces (1 cup) lemon-flavored pitted prunes, quartered

¼ cup Armagnac or other brandy

1 pint vanilla ice cream

In a small saucepan, simmer the sugar, orange juice, and prunes, stirring often to dissolve the sugar, until the prunes soften but still hold their shape, 3 to 5 minutes. Remove the pan from the heat. Immediately pour on the brandy and carefully ignite the sauce. Stir until the flames begin to die down.

Divide the ice cream among 4 dessert bowls. Ladle the warm sauce over the ice cream. Serve immediately.

COFFEE-CHESTNUT COUPE

4 SERVINGS

THIS DESSERT FEATURES FOUR of the biggest "C"s in the French repertoire: cocoa, chestnuts, coffee, and cognac. Chestnuts in vanilla syrup, also called *marrons glacés*, are available in jars or cans in many supermarkets, especially at Christmastime.

Divide the ice cream among 4 stemmed glasses, then spoon equal amounts of the chestnuts and syrup and the brandy or coffee syrup over each portion. Sprinkle each with the cocoa. Serve immediately.

1 pint coffee ice cream

1 cup chestnuts in vanilla syrup

¼ cup cognac or other brandy, or coffee syrup

2 teaspoons unsweetened cocoa, preferably European-style

PALERMO PARFAITS

4 SERVINGS

THIS FANCIFUL CONCOCTION of ice cream layered with crisp almond biscotti, dried fruits, herbal Strega liqueur, and dark chocolate is a fine illustration of the sweets of my family's Sicilian homeland, which are far more elaborate than the lifestyles of the people. My grandmother made this dessert long before quick cooking was fashionable.

8 purchased almond biscotti

½ cup diced mixed dried fruits

¾ cup Strega, Sambuca, or other anise liqueur

1 pint vanilla ice cream or frozen yogurt

2 ounces bittersweet or semisweet chocolate, shaved or coarsely grated

Place the biscotti in a heavy zipper-lock plastic bag. Crush with a rolling pin. (Don't use a food processor; it crushes them too finely.) In a small bowl, soak the dried fruits in ¼ cup of the liqueur for 10 minutes.

Divide half of the crumbs, then ¼ cup of the liqueur, then half of the ice cream among each of 4 brandy snifters or other stemmed goblets. Add all the dried fruit and soaking liquid, then make a layer of the remaining crumbs, the remaining ¼ cup liqueur, and a final layer of the remaining ice cream. Sprinkle with the chocolate. Serve immediately or cover and freeze for up to 2 hours before serving.

Goober Pies

3 SERVINGS, MAKES 6 SMALL
ICE CREAM SANDWICHES

IF YOU LIVE IN THE SOUTH, you probably already know that goobers are another name for peanuts. This combination of peanuts, chocolate, and ice cream is a sure winner.

⅓ cup chopped roasted salted cocktail peanuts

1½ cups vanilla ice cream, barely softened

12 chocolate wafer cookies (about one-third of a 9-ounce package)

Place the chopped peanuts on a plate. Spoon 2 heaping tablespoons of the ice cream onto the flat side of 1 cookie. Place the flat side of another cookie onto the ice cream and gently press until the ice cream spreads to the edge of the sandwich. Smooth the ice cream, then roll the ice cream edges in the peanuts to coat completely. Place the sandwich on a baking sheet and set it in the freezer. Repeat to form a total of 6 sandwiches, adding each to the baking sheet in the freezer.

Freeze for at least 15 minutes or up to 4 hours. If you wish to freeze longer, wrap each sandwich in a small piece of plastic wrap. Serve frozen.

COOKIES AND CREAM FRUIT PARFAITS

4 SERVINGS

1 pound ripe fresh fruit

2-4 tablespoons granulated sugar to taste

2 tablespoons liquor, liqueur, or fruit syrup

2 teaspoons lemon juice

1 cup crumbled cookies

1 pint ice cream

Peel and pit the fruit, if necessary. Coarsely dice or thinly slice the fruit and place in a bowl; you should have about 2 cups. Stir in the sugar (the exact amount depends upon the sweetness of the fruit), liquor or liqueur or syrup, and lemon juice. Let stand 20 minutes at room temperature or refrigerate for up to 1 hour, stirring occasionally to dissolve the sugar.

Spoon about one-third of the fruit into the bottom of 4 parfait or wine goblets. Sprinkle each with about 1 tablespoon of the crumbled cookies, then add scoops of ice cream, using about half of the ice cream. Make another layer in the same way, then top the ice cream with remaining fruit and the remaining crumbled cookies. Serve immediately.

- apricots, amaretto or almond syrup, coffee ice cream, biscotti

- peaches, marsala or peach nectar, pistachio ice cream, amaretti cookies

- nectarines, brandy or peach nectar, vanilla ice cream, crisp oatmeal cookies

- pears, Poire William or pear nectar, chocolate ice cream, chocolate wafer cookies

- plums, Madeira or sherry, vanilla ice cream, nut shortbread cookies

- dark sweet cherries, kirsch, chocolate ice cream, almond wafer cookies

- figs, Sambuca or anisette or anise syrup, vanilla ice cream, biscotti

- small blueberries, crème de cassis or black currant syrup, vanilla ice cream, gingersnaps

- blackberries, brandy, vanilla ice cream, vanilla wafers

- pineapple, tequila, lime sherbet, coconut macaroons

- mango, rum, passion fruit sorbet, coconut macaroons

- bananas, Cointreau or orange syrup or thawed frozen orange juice concentrate, chocolate ice cream, gingersnaps

- strawberries, Grand Marnier or orange syrup or thawed frozen orange juice concentrate, vanilla ice cream, almond macaroons

My inspiration came from a creation by Maida Heatter, the acknowledged diva of desserts. The "posies" look fabulous and fancy, but they're actually easy to make. You just spread some melted chocolate in a circle on a piece of waxed paper, put a small scoop of ice cream in the center, and gather the chocolate-lined paper around the ice cream. After just a few minutes in the freezer, the chocolate peels away easily to reveal a chocolate bouquet with an ice-cream center. I've used strawberry and pistachio flavors, but you can design your garden any way you like — "fertilizing" with chopped candied ginger or "watering" with a little cognac.

1 cup strawberry ice cream

1 cup pistachio ice cream

9 ounces (1½ cups) semisweet chocolate chips

1 bunch fresh mint

Ice Cream Posies

4 SERVINGS

Cut 8 five-inch squares of waxed paper. Place on a large baking sheet. Line a small baking sheet with waxed paper. Scoop out 4 balls of each flavor of ice cream, using about ¼ cup for each ball. Place the balls on the small baking sheet and freeze for at least 10 minutes.

Meanwhile, in a small bowl set over simmering water or in a microwave oven, gently heat the chocolate until it is nearly melted (1 to 1½ minutes in a microwave). Remove from the heat and stir until smooth. Spoon out about 1½ tablespoons of chocolate onto each waxed paper square. Working quickly, spread into rough 4-inch circles. Place 1 of the scoops of ice cream in the center of each circle, then quickly lift up the sides of the waxed paper squares and press around the ice cream ball like the petals of a flower. Freeze until the chocolate is hardened, at least 10 minutes. (The hardened "flowers" can be wrapped in plastic and frozen for up to 2 days.)

To serve, carefully peel the waxed paper off of each flower. Make beds of mint leaves on each of 4 dessert plates. Arrange 2 flowers on each plate. Serve immediately. (If the flowers have been frozen for more than 3 hours, let them stand for 5 minutes before serving.)

BLUEBERRY WAFFLE ICE CREAM SANDWICHES

4 SERVINGS

THIS IS A TERRIFIC DESSERT for any season. Although fresh blueberries make an outstanding sauce, the recipe is nearly as good when made with frozen berries, which are often more flavorful than some of the supposedly fresh berries in the market. Pizzelles, or Italian waffle cookies, which are usually lightly flavored with anise, are widely available in supermarkets and Italian grocery stores.

In a medium nonreactive saucepan over medium heat, simmer half of the blueberries with the sugar, lemon juice, and 2 tablespoons water, stirring often, until they pop and release their juices, about 5 minutes. Simmer, stirring often, until the sauce is slightly thickened, about 2 minutes more. Remove from the heat and stir in the remaining blueberries and the crème de cassis, syrup, or orange juice. Let cool slightly. (The sauce can be refrigerated for up to 2 days. Reheat gently before serving.)

Place 1 pizzelle on each of 4 dessert plates. Top with the ice cream, then place the remaining pizzelles on the ice cream, pressing down slightly, to form a sandwich. Spoon the blueberry sauce over the top of each pizzelle. Serve immediately.

3 cups fresh blueberries or a 12-ounce package of unsweetened frozen blueberries, thawed

¼ cup granulated sugar

1 tablespoon lemon juice

2 tablespoons crème de cassis, black currant syrup, or orange juice

8 purchased pizzelle cookies, each 3-4 inches in diameter

1 pint vanilla ice cream

ESPRESSO BAKED ALASKA

4 SERVINGS

4 slices purchased pound cake, each about 1 inch thick and about 4 inches square

4 tablespoons coffee liqueur, such as Kahlua, or coffee syrup

1 pint premium espresso or dark coffee ice cream

4 large egg whites, at room temperature

½ cup granulated sugar

Place the pound cake slices on a metal baking sheet, leaving at least 4 inches between each. Drizzle or brush each slice with 1 tablespoon of the liqueur or syrup. Place a large scoop or 2 medium scoops of ice cream on top of each slice of pound cake. Place the baking sheet in the freezer for at least 20 minutes or up to 4 hours.

Preheat the oven to 450 degrees. In a large mixing bowl, beat the egg whites on medium speed until they begin to mound. Raise the speed to high and beat in the sugar, 1 tablespoon at a time, until the egg whites form stiff peaks, about 5 minutes total.

Spread the meringue over each ice cream and cake portion, covering completely and using the back of a spoon to make large mounds and swirls. Immediately place in the oven and bake until the meringue is delicately browned, 4 to 5 minutes. Use a spatula to transfer the Alaskas to 4 dessert plates. Serve immediately.

Fools, Mousses, and Cool Custards

WHEN MY YOUNGEST SON WAS ABOUT FIVE YEARS OLD, HE SHOOK THE HAND OF OUR PRIEST AS we walked out of Mass one Sunday morning, then promptly invited him for dinner because his mom was making her great chocolate "mouse." The good pastor told my son that he loved mouse and that he would be right on time.

From saint to sinner, everyone loves chocolate mousse, a dessert that is satiny smooth and decadent, while maintaining the appearance of demure simplicity. Topped with nothing more than a dollop of whipped cream, a mousse is the essence of subtle sophistication. Fortunately, it is also very easy to make.

Traditional mousses rely on an egg-yolk custard base, beaten egg whites, and whipped cream. I much prefer the lightness and clearer flavors of chocolate, nut, and fruit mousses without the egg base. Eliminating the eggs also pares down the preparation to melting chocolate or pureeing fruit, then folding in whipped cream. The versatile mousse can also be layered with fruit, cookies, or cake to make elaborate but amazingly quick trifles.

Fools, old-fashioned English desserts, are even easier than mousses, and they, too, rely on whipped cream. The base is always a light fruit puree, which is partially folded into the cream to create the trademark swirled or marbled effect. Traditionally, fools are made with gooseberries, but I've expanded the concept to all sorts of readily available fresh-fruit purees and jams.

Whipping is also the basic technique for the elegant and impressive French sabayon and its Italian cousin, zabaglione, which take only a little more time than fools to prepare. Egg yolks and an acidic liquid, such as wine, are whisked into a frothy foam that can be enjoyed warm or cooled and enriched with whipped cream.

Because of their simplicity, these desserts depend upon superior ingredients. Use heavy, not whipping, cream, the best chocolate, and ripe fruits. Then present your creation in your finest china or crystal. Chocolate mousse after dinner is a special event, no matter how old you are.

RHUBARB FOOL

4 SERVINGS

Place the rhubarb, sugar, and orange juice in a large saucepan. Bring to a simmer over medium heat, stirring to dissolve the sugar. Cover the pan, reduce the heat to medium-low, and simmer until the rhubarb is very soft, about 6 minutes. Remove from the heat and stir in the orange liqueur or syrup. Transfer to a bowl and refrigerate until chilled, at least 15 minutes or for up to 24 hours.

To assemble the fool, alternate layers of the rhubarb mixture and the yogurt in 4 large wine goblets. Use a small knife to gently swirl the top layers of fruit and yogurt together. Serve immediately or refrigerate for up to 1 hour.

WHEN WE MOVED TO OUR 1761 colonial farmhouse, the only vestige of a once prolific garden was a single hearty rhubarb plant that grew big and bushy among the many weeds. In the two decades since then, I've carefully planned and planted many gardens but have left that sturdy rhubarb plant undisturbed. It still yields ruby red stalks every spring, which I make into this lovely, low-fat version of a classic English fruit dessert. If fresh rhubarb is out of season, frozen is a fine substitute.

1 pound fresh rhubarb stalks, trimmed and cut crosswise into ½-inch slices, or 1-pound bag frozen sliced rhubarb, thawed

½ cup granulated sugar

6 tablespoons orange juice

¼ cup orange liqueur, such as Grand Marnier or Cointreau, or orange syrup

2 cups vanilla yogurt

1 cup heavy cream, chilled

1 cup flavored fruit puree

FOOL'S RAINBOW

4 SERVINGS

Whip the cream to very firm peaks in a mixing bowl. Spoon a small dollop of whipped cream into 4 stemmed goblets. Add about half of the fruit puree, then half of the remaining cream. Make another layer of each to use the remaining fruit and cream.

Use a table knife to gently swirl the fruit and cream, creating a marbled effect. Serve immediately or refrigerate for up to 30 minutes before serving.

RED RASPBERRY: In a food processor or blender, puree a 10-ounce package (about 2 cups) partially thawed frozen raspberries with 2 tablespoons raspberry jam, 2 tablespoons kirsch, raspberry liqueur or raspberry syrup, and 2 tablespoons powdered sugar. Strain, pushing the puree through the sieve with the back of a spoon.

BLACKBERRY: In a food processor or blender, puree 2 cups fresh or partially thawed frozen blackberries with 2 tablespoons black raspberry or currant preserves, 2 tablespoons crème de cassis or black currant syrup, and 2 tablespoons powdered sugar. Strain, pushing the puree through the sieve with the back of a spoon.

APPLESAUCE: Stir together 1 cup thick, smooth applesauce and 2 tablespoons Calvados or applejack or apple cider.

APRICOT: Drain a 15-ounce can of apricot halves packed in juice, then puree in a food processor or blender with 2 tablespoons amaretto or almond syrup, 1½ tablespoons apricot jam, and 2 teaspoons lemon juice.

GOOSEBERRY FOOL

6 SERVINGS

I FIRST TASTED GOOSEBERRY fool at the famed Ballymaloe House in County Cork. Gooseberries, tart pale green berries that must be cooked before you eat them, have a short season in Ireland and are rarely seen in America. But gooseberry preserves are available in many supermarkets, and they make a marvelous fool. So do other preserves, especially ginger or Morello cherry. Because the ingredients are so few, choose a good-quality preserve.

¾ cup gooseberry preserves

1 tablespoon brandy or orange juice

1 cup heavy cream, chilled

Stir the preserves and brandy or orange juice together. Whip the cream in a mixing bowl.

Spoon a small dollop of whipped cream into the bottom of 6 parfait or stemmed dessert dishes. Make a layer of about half of the preserves, then spread on about half of the remaining cream. Add the rest of the preserves, then top with the rest of the cream. Use a small knife or thin spatula to create a marbled effect. Serve immediately or refrigerate for up to 2 hours before serving.

BERRY CRANACHAN

4 SERVINGS

Preheat the oven to 375 degrees. Spread out the oats on a baking sheet. Toast in the oven, stirring two or three times, until they are golden and fragrant, 5 to 8 minutes. Remove from the baking sheet and let cool to room temperature, about 10 minutes.

Whip the cream with the brown sugar to soft peaks in a mixing bowl, then add the whisky and whip to stiff peaks. Fold in the cooled oats. Divide 1 cup of the berries among 4 stemmed goblets. Top with half of the whipped cream, then make another layer of berries and whipped cream. Refrigerate for about 10 minutes, or cover and refrigerate for up to 3 hours before serving.

THIS IS A TRADITIONAL dessert from the Scottish Highlands, where the oats and whisky are first-rate. Toasted oats are folded into whipped cream and, within minutes, the oats begin to absorb the cream. The result is a nutty mousse that is both good-looking and good-tasting when layered with fresh berries. Nearly any berry can be used, but I especially like blackberries. Serve the mousse accompanied by good buttery shortbread cookies, homemade or purchased.

¼ cup old-fashioned or steel-cut oats

1 cup heavy cream, chilled

3 tablespoons packed light brown sugar

2 tablespoons Scotch whisky

2 cups blackberries or raspberries or a combination of any berries of your choice

BLUSHING PEACH KISSEL

4 SERVINGS

1 pound (3-4) ripe peaches

⅓ cup granulated sugar

1½ tablespoons cornstarch

¾ teaspoon ground mace

1½ cups blush or rosé wine

Drop the peaches into a pan of boiling water for about 15 seconds to loosen the skins. Use a small knife to slip off the skins. Pit and slice the peaches, reserving 4 slices for garnish (sprinkle with a little lemon juice if not using within 15 minutes). Puree the remaining peaches in a food processor.

In a medium saucepan, stir together the sugar, cornstarch, and ½ teaspoon of the mace. Stir in the peach puree, combining thoroughly, then stir in the wine. Cook, stirring constantly, over medium heat until the mixture comes to a boil and is slightly thickened, 3 to 5 minutes.

If you wish to serve the kissel right away, spoon it into a mixing bowl set over a larger bowl of ice cubes and stir once or twice until cooled. Serve immediately or refrigerate for up to 4 hours, removing from the refrigerator 15 minutes before serving. Divide the kissel among 4 dessert bowls and garnish with the reserved peach slices and a sprinkling of the remaining ¼ teaspoon mace.

LEMON BLUEBERRY CLOUD

6 SERVINGS

Grate 2 teaspoons of the colored part of the peel from the lemon and squeeze 1 tablespoon juice. In a medium bowl, gently stir together the lemon curd, mace, lemon peel, and juice. Whip the cream until just stiff in a mixing bowl. Fold three-fourths of the whipped cream into the lemon curd, then fold in all but about ¼ cup of the blueberries.

Spoon the mousse into 6 attractive stemmed glasses, such as champagne flutes or martini glasses. Garnish each with a dollop of the remaining whipped cream and sprinkle with the reserved berries. Serve immediately, or refrigerate for up to 1 hour.

1 lemon

1 cup prepared lemon curd

⅛ teaspoon ground mace

1 cup heavy cream, chilled

2 cups fresh blueberries, preferably Maine wild berries

6 ounces cream cheese

¼ cup honey

2 tablespoons lemon juice

1 cup heavy cream, chilled

3 nectarines, coarsely diced

1¼ cups crumbled gingersnap cookies

HONEY NECTARINE CHEESECAKE MOUSSE

6 SERVINGS

In a large mixing bowl, with an electric mixer, blend the cream cheese, honey, and lemon juice until smooth. Add the cream and whip the mixture to very firm peaks. Fold in about three-fourths of the nectarines and 1 cup of the gingersnaps.

Spoon the mixture into a 2-quart dessert bowl or into 6 individual dishes. Sprinkle with the remaining diced nectarines and crumbled cookies. Serve immediately or refrigerate for up to 3 hours before serving.

BITTERSWEET CHOCOLATE MOUSSE WITH PEARS

4 SERVINGS

In a small bowl set over a pan of simmering water, or in a microwave oven, gently heat the chocolate with 2 tablespoons of the cream until nearly melted (about 1 minute in the microwave). Remove from the heat and stir until smooth. Let cool a few minutes, then stir in 2 tablespoons of the liqueur or nectar.

In a mixing bowl, whip the remaining cream to stiff peaks. Spoon the chocolate mixture over the whipped cream and use a spatula to fold gently until no streaks of white remain. Refrigerate the mousse for 15 minutes or cover and chill for up to 6 hours before serving.

When you are ready to serve, divide the mousse among 4 dessert plates, placing a dollop in the center of each. Arrange the pear slices in a fan around the mousse. Drizzle the pears with the remaining 2 tablespoons of liqueur or nectar.

BITTERSWEET CHOCOLATE AND ripe sweet pears are a great combination, especially in autumn. In winter, change the liqueur to Grand Marnier and substitute tangerines. Amaretto and strawberries work well in spring, light rum and peaches in summer. Or serve the mousse without any fruit at all — flavor with Kahlúa and top with a little sweetened whipped cream.

6 ounces bittersweet chocolate, chopped, or 1 cup semisweet chocolate chips

1 cup heavy cream, chilled

4 tablespoons Poire William or brandy, or canned pear nectar

4 small ripe pears, cored and sliced

WHITE CHOCOLATE MOUSSE makes a rich yet delicate springtime dessert when spooned into stemmed glasses or champagne flutes and topped with a few berries, but it is really spectacular when served in edible chocolate liqueur cups, which are available in candy stores and many supermarkets. This recipe will also fill 4 to 6 standard chocolate shells.

6 ounces (1 cup) white chocolate chips or white chocolate, chopped

1 cup heavy cream

2 tablespoons raspberry liqueur, such as Framboise, or raspberry syrup

18-24 chocolate liqueur cups or 4-6 chocolate dessert shells (3-4 inches in diameter)

½ pint fresh raspberries

RASPBERRY-WHITE CHOCOLATE DEMITASSE

MAKES 18 TO 24 DEMITASSE CUPS

In a small bowl set over a pan of simmering water, or in a microwave oven, gently heat the chocolate with ¼ cup of the cream until nearly melted (about 1 minute in a microwave). Refrigerate the remaining cream. Remove the chocolate mixture from the heat and stir until smooth. Place in the refrigerator for about 5 minutes, stirring once or twice, until cooled. Stir in the liqueur or syrup.

In a mixing bowl, whip the remaining ¾ cup cream to stiff peaks. Spoon the chocolate mixture over the whipped cream and use a spatula to fold gently until smooth. Refrigerate for 15 minutes to firm the mousse slightly. (The mousse can be made up to 4 hours ahead.)

Use a small spoon to fill the chocolate liqueur cups or dessert shells with the mousse and sprinkle the tops with the raspberries. Serve immediately or refrigerate for up to 1 hour before serving.

PEANUT BUTTER MOUSSE

6 TO 8 SERVINGS

PEANUT BUTTER PURISTS WILL find no need to embellish this rich mousse, though a few shavings of bittersweet chocolate wouldn't hurt. You can choose smooth, chunky or reduced-fat peanut butter (which I actually prefer for its sharper taste) and use skim milk. Any way you make it, this dessert is an indulgence.

In a small saucepan, bring the milk to a simmer. Place the peanut butter chips in a medium mixing bowl. Pour the hot milk over the chips, let stand for about 30 seconds, then stir until the chips are melted and the mixture is smooth. Add the peanut butter and stir just until smooth. Refrigerate for a few minutes until cooled.

Whip the cream in a medium bowl. Fold it into the peanut butter mixture. Spoon the mousse into 6 dessert bowls or glasses. Refrigerate for at least 15 minutes or for up to 6 hours. Just before serving, sprinkle with the shaved chocolate, if desired.

⅔ cup milk

10 ounces (1⅔ cups) peanut butter chips

½ cup peanut butter, smooth or chunky, at room temperature

1 cup heavy cream, chilled

¼ cup shaved or coarsely grated bittersweet chocolate (about 2 ounces), optional

CHOCOLATE HAZELNUT MOUSSE

6 TO 8 SERVINGS

4 ounces unsweetened chocolate, chopped

1½ cups heavy cream

½ cup Nutella or other hazelnut chocolate spread, at room temperature

1 cup marshmallow fluff

6 tablespoons chopped skinned hazelnuts (see page 34)

In a medium bowl set over a pan of simmering water, or in a microwave oven, gently heat the chocolate with ½ cup of the cream until it is nearly melted (about 45 seconds in a microwave). Refrigerate the remaining cream. Remove the chocolate mixture from the heat and stir until melted and smooth. Stir in the Nutella until smooth, then fold in the marshmallow fluff just until it is incorporated. Refrigerate for a few minutes until cooled.

Whip the remaining 1 cup of cream in a large bowl. Fold it into the chocolate hazelnut base. Spoon into individual serving bowls and sprinkle with the chopped hazelnuts. Serve immediately or refrigerate for up to 8 hours before serving.

STRAWBERRIES IN ORANGE CUSTARD

4 SERVINGS

IF YOU CAN GET LONG-STEMMED strawberries, the presentation will be spectacular. Other fruits and berries, such as apricots or blackberries, can be added to the mix or used in place of strawberries on top of the custard.

Pour the cream into a medium saucepan. Use a small knife to scrape the seeds from the vanilla bean into the cream, then add the bean. (Do not add the vanilla extract yet, if using.) Set the pan over medium heat and stir often, until bubbles form around the edge.

Meanwhile, in a medium bowl, whisk the yolks and sugar until thick and pale. Gradually whisk in the hot cream. Return the mixture to the saucepan. Reduce the heat to medium-low and cook, stirring constantly, until the custard thickens and coats the back of the spoon, about 5 minutes. Do not allow to boil.

Strain the custard into a bowl. Stir in the vanilla extract, if using, and the orange liqueur or concentrate. Set the bowl in a larger bowl filled with ice cubes and stir until cooled, about 5 minutes. Or, cover and refrigerate until chilled, at least 2 hours or for up to 24 hours. Remove the vanilla bean.

Spoon the custard into 4 shallow dessert bowls. Arrange the berries in the custard and serve.

2 cups light cream

1 vanilla bean, split lengthwise, or
   1½ teaspoons vanilla extract

4 large egg yolks

3 tablespoons granulated sugar

2 tablespoons orange liqueur, such as
   Grand Marnier or Cointreau, or
   frozen orange juice concentrate,
   thawed

20 large long-stemmed strawberries or
   1 pint strawberries

4 large egg yolks

¼ cup granulated sugar

¼ cup kirsch

1 cup heavy cream, chilled

2 teaspoons grated lemon peel

¼ cup Morello cherry or other thick
    fruit preserves

CHERRY ZABAGLIONE

4 TO 6 SERVINGS

In the top of a double boiler or a heatproof bowl, whisk together the egg yolks, sugar, and kirsch. Set the bowl over a pan of simmering water and whisk until the mixture is thick and billowy, about 5 minutes.

Remove from the heat and set the bowl in a larger bowl filled with ice cubes. Whisk often until cool, 3 to 5 minutes. Whip the cream in a mixing bowl and fold it into the cooled custard along with the lemon peel and preserves. Serve immediately in stemmed glasses or refrigerate for up to 4 hours before serving.

APRICOT ALMOND SABAYON

4 TO 6 SERVINGS

THE TRADITIONS OF ITALY AND France merge in this elegant little dessert that tastes like a billowy cheesecake, but is really a kind of instant custard. Apricots are the perfect fruit, but peaches, plums, or nectarines are lovely as well.

Toast the almonds in a small dry skillet over medium heat, stirring, for about 3 minutes until golden and fragrant. (Or toast on a small baking sheet in a 400-degree oven, stirring often, for 5 to 8 minutes.) Immediately remove them from the skillet to prevent burning.

In the top of a double boiler or in a small saucepan set over a pan of simmering water, whisk the eggs and yolk with the sugar, amaretto, and lemon juice until thick, fluffy, and ivory in color, about 5 minutes. Remove from the heat, and whisk in the mascarpone. Place the pan in a large bowl filled with ice cubes and whisk until the sabayon is cooled, 3 to 5 minutes. (The sabayon can be refrigerated for up to 1 hour. If refrigerated longer, it will thicken considerably, but taste just as good.)

To assemble the desserts, arrange the apricot quarters on dessert plates. Spoon a ribbon of sabayon over the apricots, then sprinkle with the almonds.

¼ cup sliced almonds

2 large eggs, plus 1 large egg yolk

¼ cup granulated sugar

¼ cup amaretto

1 tablespoon lemon juice

½ cup mascarpone cheese

6 large or 9 medium apricots, pitted and quartered

PINEAPPLE RUM ZABAGLIONE

4 SERVINGS

¼ cup shredded sweetened coconut

3 large egg yolks

¼ cup packed dark brown sugar

⅓ cup frozen unsweetened pineapple juice concentrate, thawed

¼ cup dark rum

Toast the coconut in a dry skillet over medium heat, stirring, until golden brown and fragrant, 2 to 3 minutes. Immediately remove from the skillet to prevent burning. (Or toast on a small baking sheet in a 375-degree oven, stirring occasionally, for 3 to 5 minutes.)

In the top of a double boiler or in a medium bowl set over hot water, whisk together the egg yolks, brown sugar, pineapple juice concentrate, and rum. Whisk until the mixture is tripled in volume, thick, and billowy, 3 to 5 minutes.

Spoon the zabaglione into 4 narrow-stemmed glasses or champagne flutes. Sprinkle the top with the coconut. Serve immediately with long-handled spoons, such as iced tea spoons.

COOKIES AND MILK CHOCOLATE MOUSSE

4 SERVINGS

THIS IS A NEW TAKE ON AN old-fashioned 1960s "icebox" dessert of wafer cookies layered with whipped cream and softened in the refrigerator. Even as a child, I liked the dessert best shortly after assembly, when the cookies retain most of their crispness.

In a small bowl set over simmering water or in a microwave oven, gently heat the chocolate until nearly melted (about 1 minute in a microwave). Remove from the heat and stir until melted and smooth. Let stand a few minutes to cool to tepid.

In a mixing bowl, whip the cream and liqueur, syrup, or nectar to firm peaks. Use a spatula to fold the melted chocolate gently into the whipped cream until no streaks of white remain.

Place 1 wafer cookie or graham cracker on each of 4 serving plates. Spoon a heaping tablespoonful of mousse onto the cookie, then overlap slightly with another cookie and then more mousse. Continue to layer the cookies and mousse in the same way, using 4 cookies for each dessert and ending each overlapping horizontal stack with mousse.

Cover and refrigerate for at least 20 minutes or for up to 24 hours before serving. (Cover the desserts with plastic wrap if refrigerating more than 1 hour.) Serve each dessert with 2 large berries on the side or with several small berries on top.

6 ounces (1 cup) milk chocolate chips

1 cup heavy cream, chilled

1½ tablespoons raspberry liqueur, such as Framboise, or other berry liqueur, or fruit syrup or nectar

16 chocolate wafer cookies (4 ounces from a 9-ounce box), or 8 whole chocolate-covered graham crackers (4 ounces), broken in half

8 large strawberries, with stems, or 1 cup small whole strawberries

CHOCOLATE TIRAMISU WITH TANGERINES

4 SERVINGS

2 ounces semisweet chocolate, chopped

½ cup heavy cream

½ cup mascarpone cheese

1 tablespoon tangerine or orange liqueur, or frozen orange juice concentrate, thawed

12 purchased soft ladyfingers, split lengthwise

4 small tangerines, sectioned and seeded

Place the chocolate in the work bowl of a food processor. In a small pan, heat ¼ cup of the cream to a simmer. With the motor running, pour the hot cream through the feed tube, processing for about 15 seconds, until the chocolate is melted and the mixture is smooth. Add remaining cream, mascarpone, and liqueur or concentrate. Process for about 10 seconds, until the mixture is smooth and light.

Spread a generous tablespoon of the chocolate-cream mixture onto the cut side of half of the split ladyfingers. Top with the remaining ladyfingers to make "finger" sandwiches. (The tiramisu can be refrigerated, covered with plastic wrap, for up to 4 hours.)

To serve, divide the tangerine sections among 4 dessert plates and arrange the "fingers" around the tangerines.

PEACH OATMEAL TRIFLE

4 SERVINGS

I LOVE THE COMBINATION OF peaches, cream, and oatmeal for breakfast—and for dessert. Made with crumbled oatmeal cookies, this quick trifle goes together in minutes. You can peel the peaches, if you like, but I rarely do if they are sweet and juicy.

In a mixing bowl, whip the cream and brown sugar to soft peaks. Add the rum or maple syrup and continue whipping to stiff peaks. Toss the peaches with the lemon juice.

In a 1½-quart deep glass bowl or 4 individual goblets or deep dessert dishes, make a layer of about one-third of the whipped cream, then about half of the peaches. Sprinkle with about half of the cookies. Make another layer of half of the remaining whipped cream, then all of the remaining peaches. Spread the top with the remaining whipped cream, then sprinkle with the remaining cookies. Serve immediately or refrigerate for up to 2 hours before serving.

1 cup heavy cream, chilled

3 tablespoons packed light brown sugar

2 tablespoons dark rum or maple syrup

1½ cups thinly sliced or coarsely diced ripe peaches (2 large peaches)

1 tablespoon lemon juice

1 cup crumbled crisp oatmeal cookies

JAMAICAN VACATION TRIFLE

6 TO 8 SERVINGS

⅓ cup sweetened shredded coconut

5-6 ounces purchased gingerbread or pound cake (half of a 10¾- or 12-ounce package pound cake)

3 tablespoons dark rum or orange juice

1½ cups heavy cream, chilled

⅓ cup canned sweetened cream of coconut

2 cups sliced or diced mixed tropical fruits, such as banana, pineapple, kiwi, and/or tangerine

Toast the coconut in a dry skillet over medium heat, stirring, until golden and fragrant, 2 to 3 minutes. Immediately remove from the skillet to prevent burning. (Or toast on a small baking sheet in a 375-degree oven, stirring once or twice, for 3 to 5 minutes.)

Cut the gingerbread or pound cake into ¾-inch cubes. Sprinkle with the rum or orange juice and toss lightly. Whip the heavy cream and coconut cream in a mixing bowl to soft peaks.

In a 2-quart glass bowl, make a layer of half the pound cake. Cover with half the fruit, then half the whipped cream. Repeat, adding layers of the remaining cake, fruit, and cream. Refrigerate for at least 15 minutes or cover and chill for up to 4 hours before serving. At serving time, sprinkle with the toasted coconut.

PERSONAL PAVLOVAS

4 SERVINGS

Crush half the berries in a mixing bowl with a fork. Add 2 tablespoons of the sugar and the liqueur or juice and stir to mix well. Let stand for 15 minutes at room temperature or refrigerate for up to 4 hours.

Reserve 4 pretty berries for garnish. Hull and slice the remaining berries or cut them in half if they are small. Peel and slice the kiwi fruits, reserving 4 slices for garnish. Quarter the remaining slices.

Whip the cream with the remaining 1 tablespoon sugar. Fold in the sliced berries and quartered kiwi slices. Place each meringue shell on a dessert plate and spoon the whipped cream into the shells. Garnish with the reserved berries and kiwi. Spoon the crushed strawberries around the meringues or pass separately to spoon onto each dessert. Serve immediately.

1 pint strawberries

3 tablespoons granulated sugar

2 tablespoons passion fruit liqueur or juice

2 kiwi fruits

1 cup heavy cream, chilled

4 individual meringue shells

Puddings and Soufflés

WHEN I WAS A NEWLYWED LIVING IN BOSTON DURING THE JULIA CHILD GOLDEN TELEVISION era, I once got a baby-sitter and spent an afternoon at a taping of "The French Chef." Julia was making a soufflé, and it fell as it came out of the oven. An incompetent cook with absolutely no self-confidence, I immediately went into a cold sweat for poor Julia. Unconcerned, she announced with her usual aplomb that she would simply serve it as a pudding. That statement was the cooking highlight of my year, and its philosophy has guided me ever since, though it would be a long time before I attempted a soufflé for guests. But now, some years and several ovens later, I've become master of my own soufflé. Usually it rises when I tell it to, but if it falls, it simply becomes a pudding—an equally worthy dessert.

In this chapter, I've included high-rising soufflés, intentional puddings, and desserts that are close cousins to both. The common ingredient throughout is the egg, inexpensive, readily available, and a powerful rising agent. For a long time, the egg was a bad guy in nutritional circles, but it has recently been redeemed and is back in our good graces. And none too soon, I say. Eggs are, after all, the basis of many quick-cooking desserts.

Both puddings and soufflés are cooked custards. A pudding, however, uses whole eggs, while for a soufflé, the eggs are separated and the whites are stiffly whipped, then folded into the beaten yolks to form an airy custard that balloons in the heat of the oven. Soufflés should be baked in deep, straight-sided dishes to encourage the batter to climb the sides and anchor the puffed tops. Individual small soufflés cook much faster than a single large one, and they are also more stable, as they each have more "side" in proportion to quivering center. Additionally, an individual soufflé makes a most impressive personal presentation.

With these recipes, your puddings will be as smooth as satin, and your soufflés will easily rise to any occasion.

Double Chocolate Pudding

6 SERVINGS

CHOCOLATE PUDDING IS comfort food at its best, and homemade pudding takes about the same time to make as does a boxed mix. The difference in taste is incomparable, especially when you double the chocolate, as I've done here. If it's a festive occasion, top the puddings with a dollop of whipped cream and a chocolate-covered coffee bean or, if you prefer, a sprig of lavender.

In a medium saucepan, whisk together the sugar, cocoa, cornstarch, and salt. Gradually whisk in 1 cup of the cream until smooth, then whisk in the remaining 1 cup cream. Set the pan over medium heat and cook, whisking constantly, until the mixture thickens and comes to a boil, about 5 minutes. Continue to whisk and boil for 1 minute.

Remove the pan from the heat and add the chocolate and vanilla. Let stand for 5 minutes until the chocolate is melted, then stir gently until the pudding is smooth. (Do not stir too much or the pudding may thin out.)

Divide the puddings among 6 small dessert bowls. Let cool for about 20 minutes to serve warm and soft, or refrigerate for at least 30 minutes or for up to 8 hours.

¾ cup granulated sugar

⅓ cup unsweetened cocoa, preferably European-style

3 tablespoons cornstarch

¼ teaspoon salt

2 cups light cream

3 ounces bittersweet or semisweet chocolate, chopped

1½ teaspoons vanilla extract

⅔ cup dark brown sugar

2 tablespoons cornstarch

2 cups half-and-half or whole milk

2 large egg yolks

1½ tablespoons unsalted butter

2 teaspoons vanilla extract

BUTTERSCOTCH PUDDING

4 SERVINGS

In a medium saucepan, whisk together the brown sugar and cornstarch. Slowly whisk in the half-and-half or milk until smooth. Set the pan over medium heat and cook, stirring almost constantly, until the mixture thickens and boils, 5 to 7 minutes. Remove from the heat and whisk about ½ cup of the hot cream mixture into the egg yolks to warm them, then return the yolk mixture to the saucepan and cook, stirring, for 1 minute, until smooth and thickened.

Remove the pot from the heat and add the butter and vanilla. Let stand for 2 minutes, then gently whisk just until blended. (Do not stir too much or the pudding may thin out.) Divide the pudding among 4 dessert bowls. Let cool for a few minutes to serve warm and soft, or chill for up to 8 hours.

Vanilla Mace Cup Custards

6 SERVINGS

Vanilla cup custards are perhaps the ultimate in rich, soothing, desserts. Use vanilla beans or high-quality vanilla extract because it, along with a dash of mace, carries the entire flavor load. Mace, a cousin to nutmeg, is a bit more mellow, velvety, and suave . . . just like this dessert.

Preheat the oven to 350 degrees. Pour the cream into a small saucepan. If using the vanilla bean, scrape the seeds into the cream, then add the bean. (Do not add the extract yet, if using.) Stir in the brown sugar. Set the pan over medium heat and cook, stirring gently and almost constantly, until the sugar is dissolved and the mixture just comes to a boil. Remove the pan from the heat.

Place the egg yolks in a small mixing bowl, then gradually whisk the hot cream into the yolks until blended and smooth. Whisk gently to avoid forming bubbles. Stir in the vanilla extract, if using, or remove the vanilla bean.

Pour the custard through a strainer into six 5-ounce (⅔-cup) custard cups, filling each equally. Sprinkle each with the mace. Place the cups in a high-sided baking pan half filled with hot water. Bake the custards in the water bath until they are nearly set in the center, 25 to 30 minutes. Remove the cups from the water bath. Let cool for a few minutes to serve warm and soft or refrigerate for up to 8 hours.

2 cups heavy cream

1 large vanilla bean, split lengthwise, or 1½ teaspoons vanilla extract

½ cup packed light brown sugar

4 large egg yolks, beaten

1 teaspoon ground mace

1½ cups half-and-half

6 tablespoons granulated sugar

6 ounces (1 cup) semisweet chocolate chips

4 large egg yolks

2 teaspoons vanilla extract

½ cup heavy cream, chilled (optional)

CHOCOLATE POTS DE CRÈME

6 SERVINGS

Preheat the oven to 350 degrees. In a small saucepan, bring the half-and-half and sugar to a simmer over medium heat, stirring to dissolve the sugar. Place the chocolate chips in a mixing bowl. Pour the hot half-and-half over the chocolate and let stand for 30 seconds, then stir until the chocolate is melted. Whisk in the egg yolks and vanilla until blended.

Divide the custard among six 6-ounce (¾-cup) custard cups or ramekins. Place the cups in a high-sided baking pan half filled with hot water. Bake the custards in the water bath until they are nearly set in the center, 25 to 30 minutes. Remove the cups from the water bath. Let cool a few minutes to serve warm and soft, or refrigerate for up to 8 hours.

While the custards are cooling, whip the cream, if using, to soft peaks. Dollop a little on each serving.

HASTY INDIAN PUDDING

6 SERVINGS

In a medium saucepan, whisk together the cornmeal and salt. Slowly whisk in the milk until smooth. Whisk in the molasses and spice. Bring to a boil over medium heat, stirring almost constantly. Reduce the heat to medium-low and simmer gently, stirring often, until very thick and creamy, 8 to 11 minutes.

Serve the warm pudding spooned into 6 dessert bowls. Top each serving with a scoop of the ice cream.

MOLASSES-SWEETENED cornmeal mush was the original quick-cooking hot breakfast cereal of colonial times, when the settlers labeled anything that used native corn "Indian." Later, Indian pudding evolved into a dessert baked for hours in a slow oven and served warm with sweet cream. This adaptation of one of America's oldest foods incorporates the quickness of the original with the sweetness of the baked dessert.

If the hot pudding is spread in a 9-inch pie plate and chilled until cold, it will become firm enough to cut into wedges. It can then be served as a simple cake that is excellent plain, but even better with a dollop of whipped cream.

½ cup yellow cornmeal

¼ teaspoon salt

2½ cups whole milk

⅓ cup molasses

1 teaspoon pumpkin pie spice

1 pint vanilla or butter-pecan ice cream

HONEY-DATE RISOTTO PUDDING

6 SERVINGS

ARBORIO RICE, WHICH COOKS to the creamy but firm consistency of a good risotto, also makes a terrific rice pudding. And like risotto, this dessert is quick to prepare and should be eaten right away. Marsala, honey, and dates provide flavorings, but other fruits, nuts, and liqueurs or juices can be added as embellishments. If you wish, top each serving with a scoop of vanilla, coffee, or chocolate ice cream.

3-3½ cups whole milk

¼ cup honey

1 cup Arborio rice

½ cup chopped dates

½ cup marsala

In a medium heavy saucepan, bring 3 cups of the milk, the honey, and rice to a boil, stirring almost constantly. Reduce the heat to medium-low and cook, uncovered, stirring often, until the rice is creamy and nearly tender, about 20 minutes. Add the dates and marsala and up to ½ cup additional milk if the rice mixture seems dry. Continue to cook, stirring often, until the rice is tender, but retains a slight chewy bite, about 5 minutes more.

Serve immediately in 6 dessert bowls.

SPICED PUMPKIN CUSTARDS

6 SERVINGS

ONE OF THE BEST THINGS about pumpkin pie is the spicy aroma that comes from the oven while the filling is baking. This recipe provides the same good smells, and making the custard alone is a whole lot easier and much quicker than baking a pie. If you want crunch, accompany it with sugar cookies or gingersnaps, and if it's Thanksgiving, add a festive dollop of whipped cream.

Preheat the oven to 350 degrees. In a small saucepan, bring the half-and-half to a simmer. In a mixing bowl, whisk together the pumpkin, eggs, brown sugar, spice, and bourbon or rum, if using. Slowly whisk the hot cream into the egg mixture until well blended.

Divide the custard among six 6-ounce (¾-cup) custard cups. Place the cups in a high-sided baking pan half filled with hot water. Bake the custards in the water bath until they are nearly set in the center, 25 to 30 minutes. Remove the cups from the water bath. Let cool for a few minutes to serve warm and soft, or refrigerate for up to 8 hours.

1¼ cups half-and-half

⅔ cup canned unsweetened pumpkin puree

2 large eggs

½ cup packed dark brown sugar

1 teaspoon pumpkin pie spice or ground ginger

2 tablespoons bourbon or dark rum (optional)

CLAFOUTI, A HOMESPUN dessert from the French countryside, is a cross between a cake and a puffy baked pudding. Though it is traditionally made with fresh cherries, readily available dried cherries eliminate the need to pit and also offer a more intense cherry essence. You can vary the recipe with other dried fruits, such as cranberries, blueberries, apricots, or prunes.

⅔ cup dried sweet or sour cherries

⅓ cup kirsch

⅓ cup granulated sugar

⅓ cup all-purpose flour

2 large eggs

¾ cup half-and-half

½ teaspoon almond extract

CHERRY CLAFOUTI

6 SERVINGS

Preheat the oven to 400 degrees. Generously butter a deep 9-inch or 10-inch pie plate. In a small bowl or saucepan, combine the cherries and kirsch. Heat in a microwave oven or on the stovetop until the kirsch is hot but not boiling. Remove from the heat and let stand for 5 minutes to plump the fruit. Transfer the cherries and any extra liquid to the prepared baking dish, spreading evenly over the bottom.

In a mixing bowl, whisk together the sugar and flour. Add the eggs and ¼ cup of the half-and-half, then whisk in the remaining ½ cup half-and-half and the almond extract to make a thin, smooth batter. Pour over the fruit. Bake until the clafouti is well puffed and a rich golden brown, about 25 minutes. Serve warm. (The clafouti will deflate if allowed to cool but will still taste delicious.)

BLUEBERRY PUFF

4 SERVINGS

LIKE A POPOVER IN A BAKING dish, this lightly sweetened, blueberry-studded batter puffs up to wildly high peaks and valleys and is served drizzled with maple syrup. The key to the high rise is to pour the batter into a hot baking dish.

Preheat the oven to 450 degrees. Place the butter in a 9-inch deep-dish pie plate and set it in the oven to heat the dish and melt the butter. Swirl the plate to cover the bottom with the butter.

In a mixing bowl, whisk the eggs with ¼ cup of the milk. Whisk in the flour, then whisk in the remaining ¼ cup milk and the sugar to make a smooth batter. Pour into the hot pie plate. Sprinkle with the berries. Do not stir.

Return the pie plate to the oven and bake until well puffed and golden, 20 to 25 minutes. Cut into big wedges and serve with the maple syrup poured over each one.

1 tablespoon unsalted butter

2 large eggs

½ cup milk

½ cup all-purpose flour

¼ cup granulated sugar

1 cup fresh blueberries, preferably Maine wild berries

½ cup maple syrup

RUM-RAISIN SKILLET BREAD PUDDING

4 SERVINGS

2 large eggs

¼ cup whole milk

2 tablespoons packed light brown
    sugar

2 tablespoons dark rum or frozen
    orange juice concentrate, thawed

4-6 slices cinnamon raisin bread

1 tablespoon unsalted butter

1 cup vanilla ice cream

In a shallow dish, whisk together the eggs, milk, brown sugar, and rum or orange juice concentrate. Soak the bread in the custard, pushing down to cover, so that all the liquid is absorbed by the bread.

Melt the butter on a large griddle or divide it among 2 skillets to accommodate all of the bread at one time. Cook the soaked bread over medium heat until golden brown on the bottom, about 5 minutes. Turn with a spatula and cook on the other side until golden brown, 4 to 5 minutes more.

To serve, cut each slice of bread into diagonal quarters and arrange on 4 dessert plates. Place a small scoop of ice cream in the center of each plate. Serve immediately.

BUTTER-PECAN BREAD PUDDING

6 SERVINGS

BREAD PUDDING WAS INVENTED centuries ago by thrifty housewives who wanted to make good use of day-old bread by soaking it in a flavored sweet or savory custard, then baking the pudding until it was softly set in the center and crusty golden on the top. I've found that baking in a shallow dish, such as a pie plate, considerably shortens the time, while keeping the integrity of this homey dessert.

Preheat the oven to 400 degrees. Generously butter a 9-inch pie plate.

Place the bread cubes in the pie plate. Sprinkle with the butterscotch chips and ¼ cup of the pecans. In a small saucepan, bring the milk and brown sugar to a simmer, stirring to dissolve the sugar. Beat the eggs in a small bowl and gradually whisk in the hot milk mixture. Pour the custard evenly over the bread. Sprinkle with the remaining ¼ cup nuts.

Bake until the pudding is puffed and crusty on top, about 25 minutes. Serve warm.

3 cups (about 4 ounces) cubed egg bread, such as brioche or challah

3 ounces (½ cup) butterscotch chips

½ cup coarsely chopped pecans

1 cup whole milk

⅓ cup packed light brown sugar

2 large eggs

⅓ cup slivered almonds

1½-1¾ cups whole milk

⅔ cup uncooked pastina

⅓ cup granulated sugar

⅓ cup sultanas or other raisins

2 tablespoons anise liqueur, such as
    Sambuca, or anise syrup

NANA'S PASTINA PUDDING

4 TO 6 SERVINGS

Toast the nuts in a dry skillet over medium heat, stirring, until they are golden and fragrant, 2 to 4 minutes. Immediately remove them from the skillet to prevent burning. (Or toast on a baking sheet in a 375-degree oven, stirring occasionally, for 5 to 8 minutes.)

In a medium saucepan, bring 1½ cups of the milk, the pastina, and the sugar to a boil. Add the raisins, reduce the heat to medium-low, and simmer, stirring often, until the pastina is tender but retains some bite and the pudding is creamy, 6 to 8 minutes. Stir in the liqueur or anise syrup, half of the toasted almonds, and the remaining ¼ cup milk, if the pasta mixture seems dry. Cook, stirring often, for 2 more minutes. Serve immediately, sprinkled with the remaining almonds, in individual dessert bowls or cups.

BURIED TREASURE COCOA SOUFFLÉS

6 SERVINGS

Preheat the oven to 375 degrees. Butter six 6-ounce (¾-cup) soufflé dishes, ramekins, or custard cups. Coat each with some sugar, tapping out the excess. Place a truffle in the bottom of each dish. In a small bowl, beat or whisk the 2 egg yolks with 2 tablespoons of the sugar until pale and thickened, about 3 minutes. Whisk in the cocoa, liqueur or coffee syrup, and vanilla.

In a large mixing bowl, beat the 4 egg whites to soft peaks with an electric mixer. Gradually add the remaining 6 tablespoons sugar and beat to firm peaks. Fold the cocoa mixture into the egg whites. Divide among the prepared dishes. Place on a baking sheet.

Bake the soufflés until well puffed, 15 to 17 minutes. Serve immediately.

SOUFFLÉS ARE MYSTERIOUS TO those who don't know how easy and practically foolproof they are to make. This one takes no more than 30 minutes, including the baking, and the results are spectacular. When your guests have eaten all but the last bit of their chocolate soufflés, they'll discover a hidden melted truffle at the bottom of the dish. Any flavor of chocolate truffle is delicious, as are buried treasures of miniature peanut butter cups or even chocolate "kisses."

6 chocolate truffles, each about 1 inch in diameter

2 large eggs, separated, plus 2 large egg whites, at room temperature

8 tablespoons granulated sugar

¼ cup unsweetened cocoa, preferably European-style

1 tablespoon coffee liqueur, such as Kahlúa, or coffee syrup

1 teaspoon vanilla extract

RASPBERRY-WHITE CHOCOLATE SOUFFLÉS

6 SERVINGS

1 cup fresh raspberries

6 ounces (1 cup) white chocolate chips

¼ cup raspberry liqueur, such as Framboise, or raspberry syrup

3 large eggs, separated, plus 1 large egg white, at room temperature

3 tablespoons granulated sugar

Preheat the oven to 400 degrees. Butter six 6-ounce (¾-cup) soufflé dishes, ramekins, or custard cups. Sprinkle each with some sugar, tapping out the excess. Divide ½ cup of the raspberries among the prepared dishes. Reserve the remaining ½ cup berries for the garnish.

In a small saucepan over low heat, combine the white chocolate and liqueur or raspberry syrup, stirring often, until the chocolate is melted, about 5 minutes. Remove from the heat. Whisk in the 3 egg yolks.

In a large bowl, beat the 4 egg whites to soft peaks with an electric mixer. Gradually add the sugar and beat to firm peaks. Fold the chocolate mixture into the egg whites. Divide among the prepared dishes. Place on a baking sheet.

Bake the soufflés until puffed and pale golden, 11 to 13 minutes. Serve immediately, garnished with the reserved berries.

PEACH-CITRUS SOUFFLÉS

6 SERVINGS

FOR SEVERAL YEARS I MADE this soufflé with dried apricots. Then one day I bought dried peaches by mistake — and what a delicious mistake that turned out to be. I tried the soufflé with dried pears and loved that version, too. You can substitute equal amounts of dried apricots or pears for the peaches. Note that this soufflé is fat-free.

In a medium saucepan, simmer the dried fruit and 1 cup water, covered, over medium-low heat, until the fruit is soft, about 10 minutes. Puree the mixture, including any liquid, along with 4 tablespoons of the sugar, in a food processor. Add the liqueur or nectar and lemon juice and process until smooth. (The puree can be prepared up to a day ahead and refrigerated. Return to room temperature before proceeding.)

Preheat the oven to 375 degrees. Butter six 6-ounce (¾-cup) soufflé dishes, ramekins, or custard cups. Sprinkle each with some granulated sugar, tapping out the excess. In a large mixing bowl, beat the egg whites to soft peaks with an electric mixer. Gradually add the remaining 2 tablespoons sugar and beat to firm peaks. Fold the fruit puree into the egg whites. Divide among the prepared dishes. Place on a baking sheet.

Bake the soufflés until well puffed and golden, 11 to 14 minutes. Serve immediately.

4 ounces (1 cup) dried peaches or apricots or pears

6 tablespoons granulated sugar

2 tablespoons orange liqueur, such as Grand Marnier or Cointreau, or canned peach or apricot nectar

2 tablespoons lemon juice

3 large egg whites, at room temperature

Speckled Banana Soufflés

6 servings

1 large, very ripe, speckled banana, peeled

1 tablespoon dark rum or orange juice

¼ cup coarsely chopped unsalted peanuts

¼ cup miniature chocolate chips

2 large eggs, separated, plus 1 large egg white, at room temperature

¼ cup packed light brown sugar

Preheat the oven to 425 degrees. Generously butter six 6-ounce (¾-cup) soufflé dishes, ramekins, or custard cups. Sprinkle each with some sugar, tapping out the excess.

In a mixing bowl, use a fork or the back of a wooden spoon to coarsely mash the banana with the rum or orange juice. Stir in the peanuts, chocolate chips, and the 2 egg yolks.

In another mixing bowl, beat the 3 egg whites to soft peaks with an electric mixer. Slowly beat in the brown sugar, 1 tablespoon at a time, until stiff but not dry peaks form. Fold the egg whites into the banana puree until blended. Divide among the prepared dishes. Place on a baking sheet.

Bake the soufflés until well puffed and rich golden brown, about 12 minutes. Serve immediately.

BRANDIED CHESTNUT SOUFFLÉS

6 SERVINGS

Preheat the oven to 400 degrees. Butter six 6-ounce (¾-cup) soufflé dishes, ramekins, or custard cups. Sprinkle each with some granulated sugar, tapping out the excess.

In a medium saucepan, whisk together the flour and 2 tablespoons of the powdered sugar. Slowly whisk in the cream until blended. Cook over medium heat, whisking constantly, until the mixture thickens and boils. Remove from the heat. Whisk in the chestnut purée and the brandy, then whisk in the 2 egg yolks.

In a large mixing bowl, beat the 3 egg whites to soft peaks with an electric mixer. Add the remaining 1 tablespoon powdered sugar and beat to firm peaks. Fold the egg whites into the chestnut mixture. Divide among the prepared dishes. Place in a 9-by-13-inch baking pan, then half fill the pan with hot water.

Bake the soufflés until well puffed and golden brown, 15 to 18 minutes. Serve immediately.

CANNED SWEETENED CHESTNUT puree is available in the baking or gourmet sections of most supermarkets, keeps well in the pantry, and provides the basis for many a quick, sophisticated dessert, especially during the winter holidays, when time is of the essence but fancy sweets are appreciated. If you have ever spent time peeling chestnuts, you won't begrudge the relatively high price of the prepared, canned variety, especially in this elegant soufflé.

1 tablespoon all-purpose flour

3 tablespoons powdered sugar

½ cup heavy cream

½ cup (about 4 ounces) sweetened chestnut puree

1½ tablespoons brandy

2 large eggs, separated, plus 1 large egg white, at room temperature

COOKIES

MY OLDEST SON'S FIRST WORD WASN'T "MOMMY" OR "DADDY." IT WAS "cookie" loud and clear. In my idealistic effort to provide him with the best (he was my first child, after all), I bought a sturdy mixer and set about making everything from chocolate chip cookies to macaroons. I once baked 40 varieties of Christmas cookies and spent an entire week assembling trays to deliver to everyone from the postman to the parish priest. I baked like that for a whole year. Then reality (and a couple more kids) set in, and I scaled back. Yet the memory of the year the house smelled like cookies still lingers. Even now, when my son and daughter-in-law come to visit, I almost always bake a batch.

But these days, I'm far more likely to mix up the dough in one easy step. Instead of creaming the butter and sugar together, I simply melt the butter in a saucepan, then cool it slightly by stirring in the sugar. I quickly whisk in the eggs, then dump the dry ingredients into the pan. This streamlined method can be applied to any number of favorites, from Tuscan Rosemary and Pine Nut Bars to Nutmeg Butter Balls to Chipotle Chocolate Bars, and to Brownie Thins. Because my cookies taste terrific when slightly warm, they are ready to eat in about 30 minutes — the same amount of time it takes to bake those artificial-tasting boxed mixes or commercial refrigerated tubes of dough!

HONEY NUT SHORTBREADS

MAKES 16 COOKIES

FOR PEOPLE WHO SAY THEY like salt better than sweet, these cookies can do double duty as cocktail nibbles or as dessert. I've made them with every nut, from pecan to cashew and peanut to walnut, and liked them all. But my favorite version uses salted mixed nuts. Honey gives these cookies a subtle sweetness.

Preheat the oven to 350 degrees. In a medium saucepan over medium heat, melt the butter. Remove the pan from the heat and stir in the honey, vanilla, and nuts. Then stir in the flour to make a stiff dough.

Spread and pat the dough into an ungreased 8-inch square baking pan. Bake until golden, firm, and browned at the edges, 22 to 25 minutes. Cool the pan on a rack for 2 minutes, then use a sharp knife to cut into 16 squares. Let the shortbreads cool in the pan for at least 10 minutes before removing them with a small spatula. (The shortbreads can be stored, tightly covered, for up to 5 days or frozen for 1 month.)

8 tablespoons (1 stick) unsalted butter, cut into 10 pieces

¼ cup honey

½ teaspoon vanilla extract

½ cup coarsely chopped salted mixed nuts

1¼ cups all-purpose flour

TUSCAN ROSEMARY AND PINE NUT BARS

MAKES 16 COOKIES

¼ cup pine nuts

8 tablespoons (1 stick) unsalted butter, cut into 10 pieces

½ cup powdered sugar

1 tablespoon chopped fresh rosemary or 2 teaspoons dried

1 cup all-purpose flour

Preheat the oven to 350 degrees. Meanwhile, spread the pine nuts on a baking sheet and place in the oven. Toast, stirring once or twice to prevent burning, until they are a shade darker and fragrant, about 5 minutes. Watch carefully; pine nuts burn easily. Remove from the baking sheet and set aside.

Meanwhile, in a medium saucepan over medium heat, melt the butter. Remove the pan from the heat and stir in the powdered sugar, rosemary, and pine nuts. Then stir in the flour to make a stiff dough.

Spread and pat the dough evenly into an ungreased 8-inch square baking pan. Bake until the bars are golden and firm at the edges, about 20 minutes. Cool the pan on a rack for about 2 minutes, then use a sharp knife to cut into 16 squares. Let the bars cool in the pan for at least 10 minutes before removing them with a small spatula. (The bars can be stored, tightly covered, for up to 5 days or frozen for 1 month.)

Maple-Oat Bourbon Balls

MAKES ABOUT 24 COOKIES

Crush the cookies in a food processor to make about 1 cup crumbs. Add the nuts to the food processor and pulse until finely chopped. Add ½ cup of the powdered sugar, the currants, maple syrup, and bourbon. Process until well combined, about 10 seconds.

Moisten your hands and pinch off pieces of dough to make ¾-to-1-inch balls. (The cookies can be made up to this point and stored, tightly covered, for up to 5 days or frozen for 1 month.) Place the remaining ¼ cup powdered sugar in a zipper-lock plastic bag. Shake the balls, a few at a time, in the powdered sugar to coat. Place in a single layer on a plate to dry for at least 10 minutes before serving. (If the cookies have been stored or frozen, dust or shake with powdered sugar before serving.)

4-6 crisp oatmeal cookies

⅓ cup pecan pieces

¾ cup powdered sugar

¼ cup dried currants

2 tablespoons maple syrup

1 tablespoon bourbon

BROWNIE THINS

MAKES 16 COOKIES

TRUTH IN ADVERTISING: these brownies are thin, but they won't make you thin. They have a more crisp, crackly texture than traditional chewy or cakey brownies. While still warm from the oven, they will be soft and rich. At room temperature, they will be fudgy. When chilled, they will be dense and chewy. Be sure to use a metal pan, not a Pyrex dish, for baking them. It makes a real difference in the quality of the crust and the texture.

4 tablespoons (½ stick) unsalted butter, cut into 6 pieces

2 ounces unsweetened chocolate, broken into small pieces

⅔ cup granulated sugar

1 teaspoon vanilla extract

1 large egg

⅓ cup all-purpose flour

Preheat the oven to 350 degrees. Coat an 8-inch square metal baking pan with nonstick oil spray. In a medium saucepan over medium-low heat, stir the butter and chocolate until both are nearly melted. Remove the pan from the heat and stir until completely melted. Blend in the sugar and the vanilla. Working quickly to prevent curdling, whisk in the egg. Stir in the flour to make a smooth batter.

Spread the batter in the prepared pan. Bake until the edges begin to pull away from the pan and the center is just firm, 20 to 22 minutes. Let cool in the pan on a rack for at least 10 minutes before cutting into 16 squares. (The bars can be stored, tightly covered, for up to 5 days or frozen for 1 month.)

CHIPOTLE CHOCOLATE BARS

MAKES 16 COOKIES

PEPPER AND CHOCOLATE MAY seem to be an unlikely combination, but a pinch of pepper makes chocolate dishes taste even more chocolatey. Here, chipotle chilies, which are smoked jalapeño peppers that can be purchased canned in spicy adobo sauce, intensify the chocolate flavor and add a tiny kick of mysterious heat.

Preheat the oven to 350 degrees. Coat an 8-inch square baking pan with nonstick oil spray. In a medium saucepan over medium heat, stir the butter and chocolate until both are nearly melted. Remove from the heat and stir until completely melted. Blend in the sugar, chipotles and adobo sauce, and vanilla. Working quickly to prevent curdling, whisk in the egg. Stir in the flour to make a smooth batter.

Spread the batter in the prepared pan. Bake until the edges pull away from the sides of the pan and the center is just firm, 20 to 25 minutes. Let cool in the pan on a rack for at least 10 minutes before cutting into 16 squares. (The bars can be stored, tightly covered, for up to 3 days or frozen for up to 1 month.)

4 tablespoons (½ stick) unsalted butter, cut into 8 pieces

3 ounces bittersweet chocolate, coarsely chopped

⅓ cup granulated sugar

1 teaspoon finely chopped canned chipotles, plus 1 teaspoon of the adobo sauce

1 teaspoon vanilla extract

1 large egg

⅓ cup all-purpose flour

Golden Blondies

MAKES 16 COOKIES

> THOUGH THEY CAN BE DRESSED up with nuts, I don't think these moist and tender golden bar cookies need any adornment at all. They are baked at a slightly higher temperature than most blondies, giving the tops, sides, and bottoms a deep golden caramel edge.

6 tablespoons (¾ stick) unsalted butter, cut into 8 pieces

1 cup packed light brown sugar

1 teaspoon vanilla extract

2 large eggs

¾ cup all-purpose flour

1 teaspoon baking powder

Preheat the oven to 375 degrees. Coat an 8-inch square baking pan with nonstick oil spray. In a medium saucepan over medium heat, melt the butter with the brown sugar until smooth and bubbly. Remove from the heat and let stand for 3 minutes, then stir in the vanilla. Working quickly to prevent curdling, whisk in the eggs. Stir in the flour and baking powder to make a thick batter.

Spread the batter in the prepared pan. Bake until the bars are rich golden brown, crusty at the edges, and just firm in the center, 22 to 25 minutes. Let cool in the pan for at least 10 minutes before cutting into 16 squares. (The bars can be stored, tightly covered, for up to 3 days or frozen for 1 month.)

TOFFEE BARS

THE ENDURING CANDY-BAR flavor combination of crisp, buttery toffee and milk chocolate is equally appealing in a shortbread cookie. Now that toffee chips are readily available, this recipe has become my favorite for quick bar cookies. I'm sure that they will stay fresh for at least five days, but I've had a hard time keeping any around that long to prove it.

8 tablespoons (1 stick) unsalted butter, cut into 10 pieces

½ cup packed light brown sugar

1 teaspoon vanilla extract

1 cup all-purpose flour

½ cup (3 ounces) plus 3 tablespoons toffee chips, such as Heath or Skor

½ cup (3 ounces) milk chocolate chips

Preheat the oven to 350 degrees. In a medium saucepan over medium-high heat, stir the butter until it is melted, light brown, and has a nutty aroma, about 3 minutes. Watch carefully to prevent burning. Remove the pan from the heat and stir in the brown sugar and vanilla. Stir in the flour to make a stiff dough, then stir in the ½ cup toffee chips.

Spread and pat the dough into an ungreased 8-inch square baking pan. Bake until golden brown, about 20 minutes. Place the pan on a rack. Immediately sprinkle with the chocolate chips. Wait 1 minute to allow the chocolate to melt, then spread over the bars to form an icing. (If the chocolate does not melt, return the pan to the oven for a few seconds, then spread.) Sprinkle over the remaining 3 tablespoons toffee chips.

Let the bars cool in the pan for 2 minutes, then use a sharp knife to cut into 16 squares. Let cool for 5 to 10 minutes more, then refrigerate for at least 5 to 10 minutes to set the chocolate before using a small spatula to remove the bars from the pan. (The bars can be stored, tightly covered, for up to 5 days or frozen for up to 2 months.)

CRANBERRY-ORANGE BARS

MAKES 16 COOKIES

8 tablespoons (1 stick) unsalted butter, cut into 10 pieces

1 tablespoon grated orange peel

½ cup dried cranberries

½ cup powdered sugar

1 cup all-purpose flour

Preheat the oven to 350 degrees. In a medium saucepan over medium heat, melt the butter. Remove the pan from the heat and stir in the orange peel, cranberries, and powdered sugar. Then stir in the flour to make a stiff dough.

Spread and pat the dough into an ungreased 8-inch square baking pan. Bake until the bars are golden and firm at the edges, about 20 minutes. Cool the pan on a rack for 2 minutes, then use a sharp knife to cut into 16 squares. Let the bars cool in the pan for at least 10 minutes before removing them with a small spatula. (The bars can be stored, tightly covered, for up to 5 days or frozen for up to 1 month.)

CRISP APPLE SHORTBREADS

MAKES 16 COOKIES

THESE CRISP SHORTBREAD squares can stand in for apple pie when time is short and fresh apples are scarce. They are also much tidier than a wedge of pie for children's lunchboxes or for out-of-hand snacking.

Preheat the oven to 350 degrees. In a medium saucepan over medium heat, melt the butter. Remove the pan from the heat and stir in the brown sugar, apples, and spice. Then stir in the flour to make a stiff dough.

Spread the dough evenly onto the bottom of an ungreased 8-inch square baking pan. Bake until the shortbread is golden and firm at the edges, about 20 minutes. Cool the pan on a rack for about 2 minutes, then use a sharp knife to cut into 16 squares. Let cool in the pan for at least 10 minutes before removing with a small spatula. (The shortbreads can be stored, tightly covered, for up to 5 days or frozen up to 1 month.)

8 tablespoons (1 stick) unsalted butter, cut into 10 pieces

½ cup packed light brown sugar

⅓ cup chopped dried apples

1 teaspoon apple or pumpkin pie spice

1 cup all-purpose flour

CHEWY GINGER SNAPS

MAKES ABOUT 18 COOKIES

½ cup all-purpose flour

¾ teaspoon ground ginger

½ teaspoon baking soda

⅓ cup dark molasses

¼ cup packed light brown sugar

1 large egg yolk

Preheat the oven to 350 degrees. Generously butter a large baking sheet. In a small bowl, whisk the flour, ginger, and baking soda until blended. In a mixing bowl, whisk or stir together the molasses, brown sugar, and egg yolk until blended. Add the dry ingredients and stir to make a sticky dough.

Drop the dough by heaping teaspoonfuls onto the prepared baking sheet at least 3 inches apart because the cookies will spread a lot during baking. Bake until the cookies have spread and are flat and beginning to darken around the edges, 9 to 10 minutes; the cookies will not be firm. Remove from the oven and let cool on the baking sheet until they are firm enough to remove, 1 to 2 minutes. (If the cookies become too firm, return them to the oven for a few seconds to soften them and then remove from the baking sheet.) Use a spatula to transfer the cookies to a rack. Serve warm or at room temperature. The cookies will harden at the edges and become chewy in the center as they cool. (They can be stored, tightly covered, for up to 5 days or frozen for 1 month.)

Brandy Snaps

MAKES 14 TO 16 COOKIES

THE TRICK TO THESE COOKIES is to grease the baking sheet generously, then to remove them as soon as they are firm enough to slide onto a spatula—cooling takes less than a minute. Lyle's Golden Syrup, a British product available near the honey and syrup or in the specialty section in most supermarkets, is the classic liquid sweetener. Light corn syrup makes a good substitute.

Preheat the oven to 375 degrees. Generously butter a large baking sheet. In a small saucepan over medium heat, melt the 2½ tablespoons butter and the sugar together. Remove the pan from the heat and stir in the syrup and brandy. Then blend in the flour to form a smooth, thin batter. Let stand for 2 or 3 minutes to cool somewhat.

Spoon heaping teaspoonfuls of the batter onto the baking sheet at least 3 inches apart because the cookies will spread a lot during baking. Bake until the cookies are golden, lacy, and bubbling, 6 to 8 minutes. Let them cool on the baking sheet until they are just firm enough to remove with a spatula, 30 to 45 seconds. Working quickly, loosen each cookie on the sheet and transfer to a rack to cool for at least 10 minutes before serving. If any of the cookies become too firm to transfer, place the baking sheet back in the oven for a few seconds to soften the cookies. (The cookies can be stored, tightly covered, for up to 5 days. They do not freeze well.)

2½ tablespoons unsalted butter

2 tablespoons granulated sugar

1 tablespoon Lyle's Golden Syrup or light corn syrup

2 teaspoons brandy

¼ cup all-purpose flour

Nutmeg Butter Balls

MAKES 16 TO 18 COOKIES

There are many good ways to streamline recipes, but using commercially ground nutmeg isn't one of them. A nutmeg grater is on my short list of necessary kitchen gadgets, and grating fresh nutmeg takes only about 30 seconds but yields about 300 percent better flavor. If you must use commercially ground nutmeg, buy it in the smallest quantity possible so that you can use it all within a few months and then replace it with a fresh container. Once you've grated it yourself, however, there is no going back!

4 tablespoons (½ stick) unsalted butter, cut into 5 pieces

⅓ cup granulated sugar

½ teaspoon grated nutmeg

1 teaspoon vanilla extract

1 large egg yolk

¾ cup all-purpose flour

Preheat the oven to 350 degrees. In a medium saucepan over medium heat, melt the butter. Remove the pan from the heat and stir in the sugar, nutmeg, and vanilla. Working quickly to prevent curdling, blend in the egg yolk. Then stir in the flour to make a stiff dough. Let the dough cool for 5 minutes.

Pinch off pieces of the dough and form into 16 to 18 rough balls, each about ¾ to 1 inch in diameter. Place the balls about 2 inches apart on an ungreased baking sheet. Bake until pale golden, about 12 minutes. Remove from the baking sheet and cool on a rack for at least 10 minutes. (The cookies can be stored, tightly covered, for up to 5 days or frozen for up to 1 month.)

BITTERSWEET CHOCOLATE DROPS

MAKES ABOUT 2 DOZEN COOKIES

THESE EASY COOKIES COMBINE the pure chocolate of brownies with the crispness of drop cookies. If you like nuts in your cookies, stir in about ½ cup chopped pecans or walnuts.

Preheat the oven to 350 degrees. Coat a large baking sheet with non-stick oil spray. In a medium saucepan over medium-low heat, stir the chocolate and butter until both are nearly melted. Remove from the heat and stir until the chocolate is completely melted. Blend in the sugar. Working quickly to prevent curdling, whisk in the egg. Then stir in the flour and baking powder to make a stiff dough.

Drop round tablespoonfuls of dough about 1½ inches apart on the prepared baking sheet. Bake until the cookies are set and the tops are crackly, 8 to 10 minutes. Let cool on the baking sheet for about 2 minutes, then transfer to a rack. Serve slightly warm or at room temperature. (The cookies can be stored, tightly covered, for up to 5 days or frozen for 1 month.)

4 ounces bittersweet chocolate, broken into pieces

2 tablespoons unsalted butter

½ cup granulated sugar

1 large egg

6 tablespoons all-purpose flour

½ teaspoon baking powder

BISCOTTI DROPS

MAKES ABOUT 18 COOKIES

2 large eggs

½ cup granulated sugar

1 tablespoon anise liqueur, such as Sambuca, or anise syrup

1 teaspoon baking powder

1 cup all-purpose flour

1½ teaspoons aniseeds

Preheat the oven to 350 degrees. Coat a large baking sheet with nonstick oil spray. In a large mixing bowl, whisk together the eggs, sugar, and liqueur or syrup until blended. Sprinkle the baking powder over the mixture and whisk to blend. Add the flour and aniseeds, stirring to make a stiff batter. Drop the dough by tablespoonfuls onto the prepared baking sheet.

Bake until the cookies have rich golden brown edges and the centers are just beginning to color, 12 to 14 minutes. Transfer them to a rack and let cool at least 5 minutes. The warm cookies will have a cakey texture, and they will firm considerably upon cooling. (The cookies can be stored, tightly covered, for up to 5 days or frozen for 1 month.)

ITALIAN PIGNOLI MACAROONS

MAKES 16 COOKIES

Preheat the oven to 350 degrees. Line a large baking sheet with parchment paper. In a food processor, puree the almond paste with the egg white and powdered sugar for about 20 seconds until smooth, stopping to scrape down the sides of the work bowl once or twice. Drop the dough by heaping teaspoonfuls at least 1½ inches apart onto the prepared baking sheet. Sprinkle each macaroon with 5 or 6 pine nuts.

Bake until the macaroons are firm and pale gold, about 15 minutes. Slide the parchment paper with the cookies on it onto a rack to cool for at least 5 minutes, then carefully peel away the paper. Cool for at least another 5 minutes before serving. (The cookies can be stored, tightly covered, for up to 3 days or frozen for 1 month.)

CANNED ALMOND PASTE AND A food processor reduce the preparation time for this classic cookie to about one minute. While some recipes call for almond paste in cans or tubes, the canned is much more firm and the only kind that will reliably form nicely shaped macaroons. It keeps in the cupboard for a long time and has myriad uses, so invest in a can. To make almond macaroons, substitute a single whole almond for the pine nuts on each cookie.

4 ounces canned almond paste

1 large egg white

⅓ cup powdered sugar

½ cup pine nuts

2 tablespoons unsalted butter

1 large egg white

¼ cup granulated sugar

½ teaspoon vanilla extract

3 tablespoons all-purpose flour

⅓ cup sliced almonds

ALMOND TUILES

MAKES 16 TO 18 COOKIES

Preheat the oven to 400 degrees. Generously butter a large baking sheet, then dust it with flour, tapping off the excess. In a small saucepan over medium heat, melt the 2 tablespoons butter. Remove from the pan and let cool for 3 or 4 minutes until tepid.

Meanwhile, in a small mixing bowl, whisk the egg white with the sugar and vanilla. Stir in the flour, then the melted butter and the almonds to make a very thin batter. Let the batter stand for about 5 minutes.

Spoon heaping teaspoonfuls of the batter onto the baking sheets, leaving at least 3 inches in between each one. Bake until the cookies have dark golden brown edges and are cream-colored and just firm in the center, about 8 minutes. Use a spatula to carefully transfer the warm cookies to a rack to cool, or drape them over a rolling pin or thick broom handle to cool in a curved shape. (The cookies can be stored, tightly covered, for up to 5 days. They can be frozen, but they are very delicate and tend to break easily.)

Five-Spice Wonton Cookie Crisps

MAKES 16 TO 18 COOKIES

WONTON SKINS ARE ENORMOUSLY versatile and make wonderfully quick contemporary cookies. Though cinnamon, cloves, anise, or ginger are wonderful spices for the crisps, my favorite is Chinese five-spice powder, a combination of all of the above, plus fennel or licorice root. It is readily available in the spice section of good supermarkets.

Preheat the oven to 400 degrees. Brush both sides of the wonton skins with the butter. (Be sure that you are using single-ply skins — they often stick together in the package but are easy to separate.) Place them on a baking sheet. In a small dish, combine the sugar and spice powder. Sprinkle the tops of the wontons with the spiced sugar.

Bake until the wontons are crisp with dark golden edges, 5 to 7 minutes. Transfer to a rack and cool slightly. Serve warm or at room temperature. (The wonton crisps are best served within a few hours, but can be stored in a tightly covered container for a day or two.)

16-18 wonton skins (each about 4 inches square)

2 tablespoons unsalted butter, melted

2 tablespoons granulated sugar

1 teaspoon Chinese five-spice powder

THERE IS NO FLOUR IN THESE cookies, which is why they are extra peanutty and chewy. I've successfully substituted chocolate chips or peanut butter chips for the raisins, but this version is my favorite. Dried banana chips are found in bags or bulk in the fancy-snack section of the market. You can chop them in a food processor or place them in a zipper-lock plastic bag and crumble them with a rolling pin.

½ cup smooth or chunky peanut
     butter, at room temperature

½ cup packed light brown sugar

1 large egg

½ cup raisins

½ cup coarsely chopped dried banana
     chips

PEANUT BUTTER BANANA-RAISIN COOKIES

MAKES ABOUT 48 COOKIES

Preheat the oven to 350 degrees. In a mixing bowl, with a wooden spoon, blend together the peanut butter, brown sugar, and egg. Stir in the raisins and banana chips. Drop by heaping teaspoonfuls at least 2 inches apart onto a large ungreased baking sheet.

Bake until the bottoms of the cookies are rich golden brown, 10 to 12 minutes. Cool on the baking sheet on a rack for about 2 minutes, then transfer the cookies to a rack to cool for at least 5 minutes. (The cookies can be stored, tightly covered, for up to 5 days or frozen for 1 month.)

CHOCOLATE-MINT CREAM BALLS

MAKES ABOUT 24 COOKIES

DECEMBER IS THE SEASON for these uncooked delights. They take no time to make, in a month when you yourself have no time, and they taste like the essence of the holidays.

Crush the candies in a food processor to make about ⅔ cup coarse crumbs. Transfer the candy to a small zipper-lock plastic bag. Without washing the work bowl, crush the cookies in the food processor to make about 1 cup crumbs. Add the nuts and pulse until finely chopped. Add the powdered sugar, corn syrup, and crème de menthe, if desired. Process until well combined, about 10 seconds.

Moisten your hands and pinch off pieces of the dough to form ¾-to-1-inch balls. A few at a time, shake the cookie balls in the bag with the crushed candy until coated. Place in a single layer on a plate to dry for at least 10 minutes before serving. (The cookies can be stored, tightly covered, for up to 5 days or frozen for up to 1 month.)

About ¾ cup peppermint hard candies or 2-3 candy canes, broken into pieces

8-10 chocolate sandwich cookies, regular or mint (such as Oreos)

½ cup chopped pecans

⅓ cup powdered sugar

2 tablespoons light corn syrup

1 tablespoon white or green crème de menthe (optional)

Cakes

WHEN I WAS GROWING UP, ALL THE REALLY "WITH-IT" MOTHERS MADE TERRIFIC-looking, high-rising cakes from cake mixes. Boxed mixes never found their way into my mom's shopping cart, however, which increased their allure to me. One year, on the day before her birthday, I implored my father to go to the store and buy one. Mom went out to a meeting, and I went to work. An hour and a half and a splattered kitchen later, I had two magnificent-looking layers. To her everlasting credit, my mother smilingly ate two big slices and never once commented on the lack of taste.

The real lesson I learned from my cake-mix caper is that the cake took nearly as long to make and clean up after as did my mom's from-scratch recipe, and even my immature taste buds knew the difference. Since that time, I've learned how to make homemade cakes in a flash, some based on my mom's quick-and-easy specials and others that are my own inventions. All of them have few ingredients to measure, need no fussy mixing techniques, use ordinary pans, and have baking times that are far shorter than those of most standard cakes.

If you're a beginner, start with Nutmeg Crumb Cake or Blueberry Corn Cake, which are as simple as stirring dry, then liquid, ingredients together. Many of these simple cakes have so much flavor that they don't need any icing. Fragrant Gingerbread Squares, Lebanese Semolina Cake, and Hot Fudge Pudding Cake are a few examples.

These days, when I want a dessert that's a trifle more fancy, I make a cake with layers of high-quality store-bought pound, sponge, or angel food cake, something my mother would never have contemplated doing. As a result, I can now surprise her with creations like Cassata di Siciliana and tiramisu, which she enjoys with unfeigned pleasure.

Nutmeg Crumb Cake

6 SERVINGS

THIS IS A VARIATION ON A cake that my mother makes for both dessert and breakfast. The original recipe used a couple of bowls and a mixer, but I've developed a quick saucepan method. Even my mother says it has the same moist, tender texture and flavor.

Preheat the oven to 375 degrees. Coat an 8-inch square baking pan with nonstick oil spray. Melt the butter in a medium saucepan or in a mixing bowl in a microwave oven. Stir in the flour, brown sugar, and nutmeg until the mixture resembles coarse crumbs. Measure out and reserve ½ cup of the crumbs.

In a small bowl, whisk the baking soda into the buttermilk or yogurt, then whisk in the vanilla and egg yolk. Stir the liquid ingredients into the dry ingredients. Spread the batter evenly in the pan, then sprinkle with the reserved ½ cup crumbs.

Bake until golden brown and a toothpick inserted into the center comes out clean, about 25 minutes. Serve warm or at room temperature on the day of baking. (The cake may be covered and frozen for up to 1 month.)

6 tablespoons (¾ stick) unsalted butter

1¼ cups all-purpose flour

¾ cup packed light brown sugar

1 teaspoon grated nutmeg

½ teaspoon baking soda

½ cup buttermilk or plain yogurt

¾ teaspoon vanilla extract

1 large egg yolk

⅔ cup all-purpose flour

6 tablespoons granulated sugar

¼ cup yellow cornmeal

1 teaspoon baking powder

6 tablespoons heavy cream

3 tablespoons unsalted butter, melted

1 large egg

½ cup fresh blueberries

BLUEBERRY CORN CAKE

6 SERVINGS

Preheat the oven to 400 degrees. Butter an 8-inch square baking pan. In a mixing bowl, whisk together the flour, sugar, cornmeal, and baking powder. In a smaller bowl, whisk together the cream, melted butter, and egg. Stir the liquid ingredients into the dry ingredients just until blended, then stir in the blueberries. Scrape the batter into the prepared pan, smoothing the top.

Bake until the cake is firm and golden, 20 to 23 minutes. Let cool slightly, then cut into squares and serve warm or at room temperature.

GINGERBREAD SQUARES

8 SERVINGS

Preheat the oven to 375 degrees. Butter an 8- or 9-inch square baking pan. In a small bowl, whisk together the flour, spice, and baking soda.

In a medium saucepan, melt the butter with the brown sugar, stirring constantly. Remove the pan from the heat. Whisk in the molasses and orange juice, then whisk in the egg until smooth. Add the dry ingredients and blend until smooth.

Spread the batter in the prepared pan. Bake until a toothpick inserted into the center of the cake comes out clean, about 25 minutes. Let cool slightly before cutting into squares. Serve warm or at room temperature.

THE AROMA OF GINGERBREAD baking in the oven is nearly as good as the taste of the cake itself. Once, when we were trying to sell our house, I mixed up a batch before a likely buyer came to look, thinking that the good smells in our kitchen would make the house more appealing. It did. A dollop of whipped cream wasn't needed to close the deal, but it is a wonderful accompaniment to gingerbread anyway.

1¼ cups all-purpose flour

2 teaspoons pumpkin pie spice

1 teaspoon baking soda

4 tablespoons (½ stick) unsalted butter

⅓ cup dark brown sugar

⅓ cup dark molasses

½ cup orange juice

1 large egg

1½ cups semolina flour

¾ cup granulated sugar

1 teaspoon ground cinnamon

¾ teaspoon baking soda

2 cups vanilla or lemon yogurt

3 teaspoons orange flower water

1 teaspoon almond extract

LEBANESE SEMOLINA CAKE

9 SERVINGS

Preheat the oven to 350 degrees. Coat an 8-inch square baking pan with nonstick oil spray. In a medium mixing bowl, whisk together the semolina flour, ½ cup of the sugar, cinnamon, and baking soda. Whisk or stir in 1 cup of the yogurt, 2 teaspoons orange flower water, and ½ teaspoon almond extract to make a stiff batter. Spread the batter in the baking pan.

Bake until the top is golden and the cake is firm and begins to pull away from the sides of the pan, about 22 minutes.

Meanwhile, in a small saucepan, combine the remaining ¼ cup sugar with 2 tablespoons water. Bring to a boil, stirring to dissolve the sugar. Boil for 2 minutes, remove from the heat, and stir in the remaining 1 teaspoon orange flower water and ½ teaspoon almond extract.

Remove the cake from the oven (leave the oven on) and score it into 9 pieces. Drizzle the warm glaze over the cake, spreading to cover the top. Return the cake to the oven until the glaze is almost completely absorbed and the top of the cake is glossy. Let cool in the pan on a rack for a few minutes. Serve warm or at room temperature on the day of baking, topping each portion with some of the remaining 1 cup yogurt.

4 large eggs, at room temperature

¾ cup granulated sugar

1½ teaspoons vanilla extract

⅔ cup all-purpose flour

1 teaspoon baking powder

¼ cup powdered sugar

1 cup strawberry or raspberry or any
   other preserves, jam, or jelly

RED BERRY JELLY ROLL

8 TO 10 SERVINGS

Preheat the oven to 400 degrees. Line a 10½-by-15½-inch jelly-roll pan with waxed paper. In a large mixing bowl, with an electric mixer, beat the eggs until lightened in color and fluffy, about 4 minutes. Gradually add the sugar and then the vanilla and continue to beat until very thick and billowy, about 3 minutes more. Place ⅓ cup of the flour in a fine sieve or sifter and sprinkle over the batter. Use a spatula to fold it into the batter. Repeat the procedure with the remaining ⅓ cup flour, this time mixing in the baking powder.

Spread the batter evenly in the prepared pan. Bake until the top is golden and springs back when touched with your finger, 12 to 14 minutes.

While the cake is baking, sprinkle a large dish towel with about 2 tablespoons of the powdered sugar, shaking it through a small sieve or a sifter. When the cake is done, invert the pan onto the towel. Remove the pan and carefully peel off the waxed paper. Roll up the warm cake and dish towel together, starting from the short side. Let the rolled cake cool on a rack for at least 10 minutes or up to 3 hours.

Unroll the cake, removing the towel. Spread the cake nearly to the edges with the preserves. Roll up the cake again without the towel.

Place the jelly roll seam side down on a serving plate. Serve immediately or leave at room temperature, lightly covered, for up to 6 hours before serving. Just before serving, dust the top of the cake with the remaining 2 tablespoons powdered sugar.

STRAWBERRY CREAM SHORTCAKES

4 SERVINGS

1 cup all-purpose flour

9 tablespoons granulated sugar

1½ teaspoons baking powder

¼ teaspoon salt

1½ cups heavy cream, chilled

1 quart strawberries, hulled

Preheat the oven to 450 degrees. Lightly grease a baking sheet with nonstick oil spray. In a mixing bowl, whisk together the flour, 2 tablespoons of the sugar, the baking powder, and the salt. Whisk in ⅔ cup of the cream to make a soft biscuit dough.

Drop the dough onto the baking sheet to make 4 mounds, then use your hands to flatten to circles roughly 2½ to 3 inches in diameter. Sprinkle the tops of the biscuits with a total of 1 tablespoon of the sugar. Place in the oven and immediately reduce the temperature to 425 degrees.

Bake to a rich golden brown, 15 to 17 minutes. Use a spatula to carefully remove the biscuits (they will be tender) to a rack to cool for at least 5 minutes or up to 2 hours.

Meanwhile, crush half the strawberries in a food processor with the remaining 6 tablespoons sugar, then slice the remaining berries and stir them into the crushed berries. Let stand at room temperature for at least 20 minutes to dissolve the sugar and draw the juices from the berries. (The berries can be prepared up to 4 hours ahead and refrigerated.)

Whip the remaining cream to soft peaks. Use a sharp knife to carefully split the shortcakes in half horizontally. Spoon about half of the strawberry mixture onto the bottoms of the shortcakes, then replace the tops. Spoon the remaining berries over the shortcakes and add generous spoonfuls of the whipped cream. Serve immediately.

6 tablespoons (¾ stick) unsalted butter

1 large lemon

¾ cup packed light brown sugar

1 pound (12-15) Italian prune plums, pitted and quartered

3 large eggs

2 teaspoons vanilla extract

¾ cup all-purpose flour

¾ teaspoon baking powder

PLUM UPSIDE-DOWN CAKE

6 TO 8 SERVINGS

Preheat the oven to 400 degrees. Place the butter in a 9-inch round cake pan or cast-iron skillet, and place the pan in the preheating oven to melt the butter. Watch carefully to prevent burning.

Meanwhile, grate 1½ teaspoons of the colored part of the peel from the lemon and squeeze 1 tablespoon juice. Remove the pan from the oven, pour off and reserve about 2 tablespoons melted butter, then stir ¼ cup of the brown sugar and 1 teaspoon of the lemon peel into the pan until blended. Add the fruit, tossing to coat, then smooth the fruit into an even layer that covers the bottom of the pan.

With an electric mixer on high speed, beat the eggs with the remaining ½ cup brown sugar, the reserved 2 tablespoons butter, the remaining ½ teaspoon lemon peel, lemon juice, and vanilla until thick and light, about 3 minutes. Add the flour to the batter, sprinkle the baking powder over the flour, and beat just until the dry ingredients are incorporated. Spread the batter over the fruit.

Bake until the cake is a rich golden brown and the top springs back when pressed with your finger, 22 to 24 minutes. Immediately cover with a serving plate, then use pot holders to invert so the cake turns out onto the plate. Carefully lift off the pan. Put any fruit that clings to the pan on the cake. Serve warm or at room temperature on the day of baking.

FRESH PLUM PUDDING CAKE

4 SERVINGS

1 lemon

4 ripe red or purple plums, pitted and coarsely diced

¼ cup granulated sugar

2 tablespoons brandy or orange juice

4 slices purchased angel food cake

1 cup lemon yogurt

Use a small sharp knife or zester to cut thin strips of the colored part of the peel from the lemon; you should have 2 teaspoons. Squeeze 2 teaspoons juice. In a bowl, stir together the plums, sugar, brandy or orange juice, and lemon juice. Let stand for at least 15 minutes at room temperature or refrigerate for up to 2 hours.

Just before serving, toast the cake under the broiler, turning once until both sides are golden brown, 1 to 2 minutes total. Place the cake on 4 dessert plates, ladle the plums on the cake, and top with the yogurt. Sprinkle with the lemon peel.

HOT FUDGE PUDDING CAKE

8 SERVINGS

Preheat the oven to 375 degrees. Butter a 2-quart (about 9-inch-square) glass baking dish. In a mixing bowl, whisk together the flour, ¾ cup of the brown sugar, ¼ cup of the cocoa, and the baking powder. Stir in the cream and vanilla to make a stiff batter. Scrape the batter into the prepared dish, smoothing to cover the bottom.

In a small bowl, whisk together the remaining ¾ cup brown sugar and ¼ cup cocoa. Sprinkle over the batter. Pour the hot coffee over the batter. Do not stir.

Bake until the cake is dark chocolate, with sauce bubbling up through the batter, 25 to 30 minutes. Let cool slightly, then serve warm or at room temperature.

1 cup all-purpose flour

1½ cups packed light brown sugar

½ cup unsweetened cocoa, preferably European-style

2 teaspoons baking powder

1 cup heavy cream

2 teaspoons vanilla extract

1¼ cups very hot brewed coffee

1 pound (2⅔ cups) semisweet chocolate chips or semisweet chocolate bar, chopped

10 tablespoons unsalted butter

4 large eggs, at room temperature

2 tablespoons all-purpose flour

2 teaspoons instant espresso or coffee powder

1 cup heavy cream, chilled, for garnish

BAKED FUDGE CAKE

12 SERVINGS

Preheat the oven to 425 degrees. Butter a 9-inch springform pan. Line the bottom with a round of waxed or parchment paper and butter the paper. In a medium saucepan over medium-low heat, melt the chocolate and butter together, stirring until the chocolate is about half melted. Remove the pan from the heat and stir until the mixture is melted and smooth. Set aside to cool for a few minutes.

Meanwhile, in a large mixing bowl, begin beating the eggs with an electric mixer on medium-low speed until frothy. Raise the speed to high and beat until the eggs are light in color, thick, fluffy, and almost tripled in volume, about 5 minutes. Beat in the flour and espresso or coffee powder. Stir about one-fourth of the egg mixture into the chocolate to lighten it, then fold the chocolate mixture into the eggs.

Spoon the batter into the prepared pan. Bake for 17 minutes. Cool the pan on a rack for about 10 minutes, then refrigerate until just firm enough to cut, about 30 minutes. At this point, the cake will be firm and fudgy about one-third of the way to the center, and the center will be softly set like a mousse. (The dessert can be refrigerated for up to 5 days or frozen for up to 1 month.)

Serve at cool room temperature or slightly chilled. Shortly before serving, whip the cream to firm peaks. Cut the dessert into slim wedges and place a dollop of whipped cream on top of or alongside each serving.

WARM MOCHA TRUFFLE CAKES

6 SERVINGS

4 ounces bittersweet chocolate, broken into small pieces

8 tablespoons (1 stick) unsalted butter

2 large eggs, plus 2 large egg yolks

⅓ cup granulated sugar

2 tablespoons all-purpose flour

1 tablespoon coffee liqueur, such as Kahlúa, or coffee syrup

1½ cups coffee ice cream

Preheat the oven to 325 degrees. Butter six 5-ounce (⅔-cup) ramekins or custard cups. In a small saucepan over low heat, melt the chocolate and butter, stirring often, until the chocolate is nearly melted. Remove from the heat and stir until the chocolate is completely melted.

Meanwhile, in a mixing bowl, beat the eggs, yolks, and sugar with an electric mixer until the mixture is thick and pale in color, about 4 minutes. Beat in the flour, 1 tablespoon at a time. Add the liqueur or coffee syrup and the chocolate mixture and beat until light and fluffy, about 4 minutes more.

Divide the batter among the ramekins. Place on a baking sheet. Bake until the tops of the cakes are just firm and rounded and the cakes begin to pull away from the sides of the ramekins, 18 to 20 minutes. Let the cakes stand for a few minutes, then run a knife around the edges to loosen them. Invert the cakes onto dessert plates. Serve immediately with a small scoop of the ice cream placed alongside each cake.

No-Bake Ginger-Orange Cheesecake

6 SERVINGS

To BECOME FIRM, TRADITIONAL no-bake cheesecakes must be refrigerated for several hours. By spooning the cream cheese mixture into individual cupcake tins, you can get the same result by freezing them for just 20 minutes. I like the adult taste of gingersnap crumbs, but you can use nearly any cookie crumbs for the base.

Line 6 standard-sized cupcake cups with paper liners. In a food processor, crush the gingersnaps to make about 1 cup coarse crumbs. Set aside 2 tablespoons crumbs. Add the butter to the remaining crumbs and process for a few seconds to blend well. Divide the buttered crumbs evenly among the paper liners, pressing down to form a bottom crust. Place the entire cupcake tin in the freezer for 5 minutes. Do not wash the food processor work bowl.

Meanwhile, grate 2 teaspoons of the colored part of the peel from the orange and squeeze 2 tablespoons juice. Place the cream cheese, sugar, cream, orange peel and juice in the food processor and blend for 10 or 15 seconds until smooth and fluffy, stopping to scrape the sides once or twice. Remove the cupcake tin from the freezer and divide the cheesecake batter evenly among the cups. Sprinkle the tops with the reserved cookie crumbs.

Return the cheesecakes to the freezer for at least 20 or up to 40 minutes before serving. (The cheesecakes can be refrigerated for at least 3 hours or up to 1 day.)

3 ounces (6-8) gingersnaps

1 tablespoon unsalted butter, at room temperature

1 large orange

8 ounces cream cheese, cut into 8 pieces, at room temperature

⅓ cup granulated sugar

¼ cup heavy cream

12 chocolate wafer cookies (about one-third of a 9-ounce package)

8 ounces cream cheese, cut into 8 pieces, at room temperature

¼ cup granulated sugar

1 teaspoon vanilla extract

1 large egg

½ cup (3 ounces) semisweet chocolate chips, melted (optional)

LITTLE CHEESECAKES

6 TO 8 SERVINGS

Preheat the oven to 350 degrees. Line 6 to 8 (depending upon the depth) standard-sized cupcake cups with paper liners. Set a chocolate wafer in each cup. Crush the remaining cookies in a food processor, then remove from the work bowl and set aside. There's no need to wash the work bowl.

Place the cream cheese, sugar, vanilla, and egg in it and process just until smooth and fluffy, about 20 seconds. For chocolate cheesecakes, add the melted chocolate and process just until blended in.

Divide the batter among the cups. For marble cheesecakes, pour some of the chocolate on top of each cheesecake, then use a table knife to swirl the chocolate into the batter.

Sprinkle the cheesecakes with the cookie crumbs. Bake until the cheesecakes are set and lightly colored on top, about 20 minutes. Cool on a rack for 5 minutes, then gently transfer the cups to a baking sheet and set in the freezer for at least 10 minutes before serving. (The cheesecakes can be refrigerated for up to 1 day.)

PINEAPPLE RIGHT-SIDE-UP POUND CAKE

6 SERVINGS

THE REAL APPEAL OF UPSIDE-down cake is the sticky caramel fruit and sauce soaking into the warm cake. You can get great results by spooning maple syrup, pineapple, and cherry sauce over warm toasted pound cake slices. The difference is about an hour less in preparation time.

Preheat the broiler. In a small saucepan, boil the maple syrup until it is reduced to about ¾ cup, 5 to 7 minutes.

In a medium skillet, heat the butter and cook the pineapple over medium heat, stirring, until the fruit is tinged with gold, about 5 minutes. Stir in the cherries, bourbon or orange juice, and lemon juice and simmer for 1 minute. Add the reduced maple syrup and simmer for 1 minute. (The fruit mixture can be made up to 2 hours ahead and gently reheated.)

Place the pound cake slices on a baking sheet and toast under the broiler, turning once, until golden brown on both sides, 1 to 2 minutes per side. Serve the toasted pound cake with the sauce ladled over each slice.

1 cup maple syrup

2 tablespoons unsalted butter

1½ cups fresh pineapple chunks or canned pineapple in juice, drained

⅓ cup dried cherries

2 tablespoons bourbon or orange juice

1 tablespoon lemon juice

6 slices purchased pound cake, each about 1 inch thick

LEMON CUSTARD SPONGE CAKE

6 SERVINGS

6 purchased sponge cake rounds
   (5-ounce package)

3 lemons

3 large eggs

6 tablespoons granulated sugar

½ cup heavy cream

Preheat the oven to 400 degrees. Butter six 6-ounce (¾-cup) custard cups or ramekins. Place 1 sponge cake round in each cup, pushing down to fit snugly, if necessary.

Grate 1 tablespoon of the colored part of the peel from the lemons and squeeze ⅓ cup juice. In a mixing bowl, whisk the eggs with the sugar, cream, lemon peel, and juice until well blended.

Divide the custard among the cake-filled custard cups, pouring over to cover the cakes. Place the cups on a baking sheet and bake until the edges of the custards are caramelized, the tops are flecked with brown, and the custards are softly set, about 25 minutes.

Let cool for a few minutes, then serve warm or at room temperature directly from the custard cups or inverted onto dessert plates.

Raspberry Lemon Layer Cake

6 SERVINGS

Whip the cream, sugar, and liqueur or orange syrup to firm peaks; set aside. Use a serrated knife to cut the cake horizontally into 3 even layers.

Place a bottom layer of cake on a platter. Spread one-third of the lemon curd or marmalade over the cake. Top with a single layer of raspberries placed in rows, using alternating berry colors if you have them. Spread one-third cup of the whipped cream over the berries, taking care not to disturb the rows. Make another layer of cake, lemon curd, berries, and cream in the same way. Top with the remaining cake layer. Spread the remaining lemon curd or marmalade over the top of the cake. Frost the top and sides with the remaining whipped cream. Decorate the top with the remaining berries.

Serve immediately or refrigerate for up to 4 hours. To serve, use a serrated knife to cut thick slices.

MOST SPECIAL EVENTS— weddings, anniversaries, and birthdays—are commemorated with a layer cake. Homemade ones are time-consuming and difficult to make. But with high-quality prepared ingredients, such as store-bought pound cake and lemon curd, creating a delicious and beautiful layer cake takes just minutes and no skill at all. The sweetness of the golden lemon curd plays well against the brilliant raspberries as a filling for this cake, and a frosting of sweetened and spiked whipped cream turns it into a celebratory and virtually instant centerpiece.

1½ cups heavy cream, chilled

3 tablespoons powdered sugar

3 tablespoons orange liqueur, such as Grand Marnier or Cointreau, or orange syrup

1 purchased pound cake (10-to-12-ounce package)

1 cup purchased lemon curd, or ½ cup lemon or orange marmalade

3 (½-pint) baskets raspberries, preferably one each of red, black, and golden berries

1 pint strawberries, hulled

2 tablespoons granulated sugar

2 tablespoons light rum or orange juice

¼ cup strawberry jam

6 ounces purchased angel food cake (about half of a 12-to-13-ounce cake)

½ pint fresh raspberries

1 cup vanilla yogurt

Pink Angel Summer Pudding Cake

4 SERVINGS

Slice the strawberries and set half of them aside. Place the remaining strawberries in a mixing bowl with the sugar and 1 tablespoon of the rum or orange juice. Mash with a fork and let stand for 10 minutes until they are very juicy and the sugar is dissolved. Place the jam in a small bowl and stir in the remaining 1 tablespoon rum.

Use a serrated knife to slice the cake horizontally into 3 layers. Spread the jam onto 2 of the layers. Reassemble the cake, putting the slices with jam on the bottom and middle, then cut it into 8 slices. Overlap 2 slices on each of 4 dessert plates.

Stir the reserved strawberries and the raspberries into the mashed berries. (You can spread the cake with jam up to 4 hours ahead, but do not assemble the desserts until serving time.) Spoon the berries over the cake slices. Top each serving with a dollop of the yogurt. Serve immediately.

Tiramisu Angel Torte

8 SERVINGS

Use a serrated knife to cut the cake horizontally into 3 layers. In a mixing bowl, beat together the mascarpone, ¼ cup of the cream, ¼ cup of the powdered sugar, 4 tablespoons of the rum, and 1 teaspoon of the espresso or coffee powder with an electric mixer until fluffy.

Place a layer of cake on a serving plate and spread with half the mascarpone mixture. Top with another layer of cake and spread with the remaining mascarpone. Top with another layer of cake. Refrigerate.

In a large mixing bowl, whip the remaining 1¾ cups cream with ¼ cup of the powdered sugar, the remaining 2 tablespoons rum, 1 teaspoon of the espresso powder, and ¼ cup of the cocoa to firm peaks. Frost the top and sides of the cake with the whipped cream mixture. Put the remaining 2 teaspoons powdered sugar, the remaining 1 teaspoon espresso powder, and the remaining 2 teaspoons cocoa in a small sieve and sprinkle over the top of the cake.

Serve immediately or refrigerate for up to 6 hours before cutting into slices with a serrated knife.

TIRAMISU, WHICH TRANSLATES as "pick-me-up," is similar to a trifle, with coffee- and brandy-soaked sponge cake or ladyfingers layered with a zabaglione-style custard filling and sweetened mascarpone cheese, then spread with whipped cream and dusted with cocoa. I much prefer this version of the Italian classic, lightened and simplified by skipping the custard completely and instead filling layers of store-bought angel food cake with sweetened espresso and rum-flavored mascarpone. The cake is iced with coffee-flavored whipped cream.

1 purchased angel food cake (10-12 ounces)

1 cup (8 ounces) mascarpone cheese

2 cups heavy cream, chilled

½ cup plus 2 teaspoons powdered sugar

6 tablespoons dark rum

3 teaspoons instant espresso or coffee powder

¼ cup plus 2 teaspoons unsweetened cocoa, preferably European-style

6 ounces (1 cup) plus 1 tablespoon miniature semisweet chocolate chips

6 tablespoons Strega, or anise liqueur, such as Sambuca, or orange liqueur, such as Grand Marnier or Cointreau

1 large purchased pound cake or sponge cake (12-16 ounces)

2 cups (15 ounces) whole-milk or part-skim ricotta cheese

½ cup plus 1 tablespoon chopped mixed dried fruit

1 cup heavy cream, chilled

CASSATA DI SICILIANA

8 TO 10 SERVINGS

In a small saucepan over medium-low heat, gently stir ½ cup of the chocolate chips with 1 tablespoon of the liqueur until the chocolate is nearly melted. (Or melt the chips with the liqueur in a microwave oven.) Remove the pan from the heat and stir until smooth. Set aside to cool slightly.

Use a serrated knife to cut the cake horizontally into 3 layers. Brush the cut sides of the cake layers with a total of 3 tablespoons of the liqueur. Drain off any excess liquid from the ricotta, then turn it into a bowl. Add ½ cup of the chocolate chips, the remaining 2 tablespoons of liqueur, and ½ cup of the fruit bits. Stir to blend well.

Place a layer of cake on a serving plate and spread with half the ricotta filling. Top with another layer of the cake and spread with the remaining filling, then top with another layer of cake. Refrigerate.

Whip the cream to firm peaks, then gently but thoroughly fold in the melted chocolate until no streaks of white remain. Spread the whipped cream over the cake to cover it completely. Sprinkle the top of the cake with the remaining 1 tablespoon chocolate chips and 1 tablespoon fruit bits. Refrigerate for at least 20 minutes or for up to 8 hours. Use a serrated knife to cut the cake into 8 to 10 serving slices.

Mocha Icebox Cake

8 SERVINGS

THIRTY YEARS AGO, MY mother made a version of this dessert by layering whipped cream and cookies in a loaf pan, then putting it in the icebox until the cookies absorbed the cream and become soft and cakey. Because I often sneaked a taste before the required overnight chilling, I've long known that the cake is even better much sooner, when the cookies and cream just begin to mingle.

4 ounces (⅔ cup) semisweet chocolate chips

1½ cups heavy cream, chilled

¼ cup powdered sugar

1 tablespoon instant espresso or coffee powder

Half of a 1-pound box of chocolate-covered graham crackers (about 15 whole crackers)

In a small saucepan set over medium-low heat, gently stir the chocolate chips with 3 tablespoons of the cream until the chocolate is nearly melted. (Or melt the chocolate with 3 tablespoons of the cream in a bowl in a microwave oven.) Remove the pan from the heat and stir until smooth. Set the chocolate icing aside to cool slightly. Whip the remaining cream with the powdered sugar and espresso powder to firm peaks.

In an 8-inch square baking pan, make a layer of graham crackers, breaking them to fit as necessary. Spread with one-third of the whipped cream mixture. Repeat, making 2 more layers of crackers and cream, then end with a fourth layer of crackers. Carefully spread the top layer of the crackers with the chocolate icing.

Refrigerate for about 30 minutes and serve when crackers are still somewhat crisp. Or cover the pan and refrigerate for at least 2 hours or up to 24 hours; the crackers will have softened into the cream. Cut into 8 pieces and use a spatula to transfer the slices to dessert plates.

Tarts and Turnovers

My Pennsylvania Dutch grandma always said that pie bakers are born, not made. She maintained that anyone could learn to make a good pie crust but that few inherit the touch for a great one. My grandma's gene seems to have passed relatively intact to her progeny, and to this day, our family reunions feature a whole table full of legendary pies—all homemade.

Our family is so fond of pies that we insist on having them for everyday occasions as well. But when I'm short on time, I unapologetically take shortcuts. My Strawberry Almond Butter Tart, for example, starts with a speedy almond-paste dough that takes just a few seconds in a food processor before it's ready to be pressed into a tart pan. Likewise, the crust for Grape-Walnut Mosaic Tart is just flour, sugar, nuts, and butter buzzed together in the processor—no delicate mixing or rolling out required.

It took a while before I could be persuaded to try a store-bought pie crust because early versions tasted like the boxes they came in. But one day a family member who shall remain nameless promised I'd bring a pie to an event but neglected to inform me until 30 minutes before, and I had no choice. That's when I discovered refrigerated pie crust disks in the supermarket. The folded rounds come separately wrapped, two to a box, and fit perfectly into a 9-inch pie or tart pan. The happy result—much to the relief of the family member who inadvertently introduced me to them—is a good-tasting, flaky crust. Similarly, frozen puff pastry is one of the better products in the supermarket freezer and saves you a day chained to a work surface painstakingly rolling, folding, and chilling the dough to create the proper million-layered flakiness.

With the pastry out of the way, you're free to focus on a whole range of homemade fillings, from country apple and Southern pecan to banana-macadamia nut. Within 30 minutes from start to finish, you can put an exquisite tart in front of family or guests.

My grandma, a very modern woman who worked every day of her life and championed the cause of any new product that made life easier without affecting quality, would approve.

STRAWBERRY ALMOND BUTTER TART

8 SERVINGS

THIS BUTTERY ALMOND CRUST is as much cake as it is pastry. Prepared in seconds with canned almond paste and a food processor, it is spread with lemon curd and covered with strawberries. If blueberries are in season, they make a wonderful replacement. If you don't have lemon curd on hand, spread the pastry with a thin layer of jam.

Preheat the oven to 375 degrees. Coat a 9- or 10-inch tart pan (with or without a removable bottom) with nonstick oil spray. In a food processor, blend the almond paste with the sugar and butter until smooth, stopping once or twice to scrape down the sides, about 20 seconds total. Add the eggs and process until well blended, about 10 seconds. Add the flour and process until blended, about 5 seconds.

Spread the dough in the prepared pan. Bake until the top is golden and springs back when lightly pressed, 20 to 25 minutes. Cool in the pan on a rack for at least 8 minutes. (The pastry can be stored at room temperature, covered, for 1 day or frozen for up to 1 month.)

Spread the top of the pastry with the lemon curd or jam. Leave the berries whole if they are small or slice them if they are large. Cover the top with whole berries, hulled sides down, or overlap the sliced berries to cover the top. Serve immediately or refrigerate for up to 4 hours before serving.

½ cup (4 ounces) canned almond paste, broken into 6 pieces

½ cup granulated sugar

10 tablespoons unsalted butter, cut into 15 pieces

3 large eggs

½ cup all-purpose flour

½ cup purchased lemon curd or ⅓ cup lemon or apricot jam or preserves

2 pints strawberries, hulled

Black-Bottom Berry Tart

4 SERVINGS

THIS TART LOOKS AS IF IT came from a fancy French bakery, but is actually one of the easiest in the book. Warm bittersweet chocolate sauce is spread in a simple baked pastry shell and covered with berries. Small strawberries make a beautiful tart, and golden and red raspberries, arranged in concentric circles make an even more dramatic presentation. Or use red and green seedless grapes and brush them with apple jelly.

1 refrigerated folded pie crust (half of a 15-ounce package)

6 ounces bittersweet chocolate, chopped, or 1 cup semisweet chocolate chips

¼ cup heavy cream

1 pint raspberries or small strawberries, hulled

2 tablespoons raspberry or red currant jelly

1½ tablespoons cognac or raspberry liqueur, such as Framboise, or raspberry syrup

Preheat the oven to 425 degrees. Ease the pie crust into a 9-inch tart pan with a removable bottom, folding in the extra pastry to reinforce the edges. Prick the bottom of the pastry 8 or 10 times with a fork. Freeze in the pan for 10 minutes.

Bake the frozen pastry until it is lightly browned, about 12 minutes. Let cool for at least 5 minutes. (The pastry shell can be stored at room temperature, covered, for 1 day.)

In a small bowl set over a pan of simmering water or in a microwave oven, heat the chocolate until nearly melted (about 1 minute in a microwave). Remove from the heat and stir until smooth. Blend in the cream. Spread the chocolate over the bottom of the tart shell. Arrange the berries, hulled side down, in the chocolate, covering completely. Refrigerate until the chocolate is set, about 10 minutes.

Melt the jelly and liqueur or syrup together in a small saucepan or microwave oven. Brush the berries with the glaze. Serve immediately or refrigerate for up to 6 hours.

FIG AND SWEET CHEESE TARTS

4 SERVINGS

CITRUS-SCENTED MASCARPONE cheese makes a lush, decadent filling for a tart topped with fresh figs—an exquisite fruit whose season is all too short and sweet. Figs remain my favorite for this elegant tart, but you can substitute other fruits, such as sliced nectarines, peaches, or various colors of grapes.

Preheat the oven to 400 degrees. Cut each pie crust in half. Ease the halves into four 4½-inch tart pans with removable bottoms. Trim the edges of the crust. Prick the bottoms with a fork. Freeze for 5 minutes.

Bake the frozen crusts until golden and crisp, 12 to 15 minutes. Remove from the oven. (The pastry shells can be stored, covered, at room temperature for 1 day.)

Meanwhile, grate 1 teaspoon of the colored part of the peel from the lemon and squeeze 1 tablespoon juice. Make a glaze by heating together the preserves, 1 tablespoon of the liqueur or orange juice concentrate, and lemon juice in a small saucepan just until the preserves melt. Remove from heat. Whisk together the mascarpone, powdered sugar, remaining 1 tablespoon liqueur, and lemon peel. (The glaze and filling can be prepared a day ahead, covered, and refrigerated.)

To serve, brush the tart shells with about half of the glaze, then spoon in and spread the mascarpone. Arrange the figs in pinwheel fashion on top of the cheese, then brush the figs with the remaining glaze. Serve immediately or refrigerate for up to 1 hour.

2 refrigerated folded pie crusts (15-ounce package)

1 lemon

¾ cup fig preserves

2 tablespoons orange liqueur, such as Grand Marnier or Cointreau, or frozen orange juice concentrate, thawed

6 ounces (¾ cup) mascarpone cheese

¼ cup powdered sugar

6 fresh figs, stemmed and quartered

1 lemon

1 pound tart apples (2-3 apples), peeled, cored, and thinly sliced

½ cup granulated sugar

1 tablespoon all-purpose flour

¾ teaspoon apple pie spice or ½ teaspoon ground cinnamon

1 refrigerated folded pie crust (half of a 15-ounce package)

1 tablespoon unsalted butter, cut into 6 pieces

COUNTRY APPLE TART

4 SERVINGS

Preheat the oven to 450 degrees. Grate 1 teaspoon of the colored part of the peel from the lemon and squeeze 2 teaspoons juice. In a mixing bowl, toss the apples with all but about 2 teaspoons of the sugar, the flour, spice, lemon peel, and juice.

Place the pie crust on a baking sheet that has been lightly dusted with flour. Dust a rolling pin with flour and roll the pastry to a rough 13-inch circle. Heap the apples on the pastry, leaving a 2-inch border all around. Scatter the butter on the fruit. Fold the pastry border back over the apples to make an uneven rustic edge of about 1½ inches, leaving the slices in the center exposed. Sprinkle the reserved 2 teaspoons sugar over the pastry border.

Bake for 12 minutes, then reduce the temperature to 425 degrees, and bake until the apples are softened and bubbly and the pastry is golden brown, 12 to 15 minutes more. Serve warm or at room temperature on the day of baking.

ALMOND PEAR GALETTE

6 SERVINGS

Preheat the oven to 400 degrees. On a large baking sheet, roll the puff pastry into a 12-inch square. Fold the edges inward ½ inch to form a double-thick border. Prick the bottom with a fork. Place in the freezer.

In a food processor, pulse to process the nuts and sugar until the nuts are finely chopped, about 10 seconds. Remove the pastry from the freezer, and sprinkle it with half the nut mixture, leaving the rest in the processor. Make rows of overlapping pear slices to cover the pastry, except for the edges.

Distribute the butter over the remaining nut mixture in the food processor. Pulse just until the butter is finely chopped, about 6 seconds. Sprinkle the nut mixture over the pears.

Bake until the pastry edges are well puffed and rich golden brown, the pears are tender, and the topping is golden, 20 to 23 minutes. Let cool slightly but serve warm.

1 sheet frozen puff pastry (17¼-ounce package), thawed but well chilled

⅓ cup sliced almonds

3 tablespoons packed brown sugar

3 medium-sized ripe firm pears, peeled, cored, and thinly sliced

1 tablespoon unsalted butter, chilled and cut into 4 pieces

SOUTHERN PECAN TART

8 TO 10 SERVINGS

1 refrigerated folded pie crust (half of a 15-ounce package)

2 tablespoons all-purpose flour

1½ cups (about 6 ounces) pecan halves

½ cup dark corn syrup

⅓ cup packed light brown sugar

2 large eggs

1 teaspoon vanilla extract

Preheat the oven to 400 degrees. Sprinkle one side of the pie crust with about ½ tablespoon of the flour. Ease the pastry, floured side down, into a 9-inch tart pan with a removable bottom, folding in the extra pastry to reinforce the edges. Sprinkle the pecans in a single layer on the bottom of the crust. Use your hands to gently pat the nuts onto the pastry. Place the pan in the freezer while you make the filling.

In a mixing bowl, whisk together the corn syrup, brown sugar, and remaining 1½ tablespoons flour. Whisk in the eggs and vanilla until blended. Pour the filling evenly over the nuts.

Bake the tart until the filling is firm, the pastry is golden, and the nuts are toasted, 22 to 25 minutes. Let cool on a rack for at least 15 minutes before serving warm or at room temperature. (The tart is best served on the day of baking, but it can be refrigerated overnight, then returned to room temperature for serving.)

Grape-Walnut Mosaic Tart

8 SERVINGS

THE SLIGHT BITTERNESS OF walnuts in the rich crust plays beautifully against the sweetness of glazed grapes in this autumnal tart. Green, red, or purple grapes all work well; I like to design a mosaic of the three. You can bake the crust ahead, but assemble the tart within a few hours of serving to keep the crisp edge to the crust. If you can get black walnuts, they are sublime.

Preheat the oven to 400 degrees. In a food processor, pulse to process the flour, nuts, and brown sugar until the nuts are finely chopped but not oily, about 10 seconds. Distribute the butter over the nut mixture. Process just until the dough clumps together. Use your hands to press the dough evenly onto the bottom and sides of a 9-inch round tart pan with a removable bottom. Prick the bottom with a fork. Freeze for at least 10 minutes and up to 2 hours.

Bake the frozen tart shell until golden brown, about 20 minutes. Cool on a rack for at least 15 minutes to firm the crust. (The tart shell can be stored at room temperature, covered, for 1 day.)

In a small pan or in a bowl in a microwave, melt the jam. Brush about 2 tablespoons of the jam on the bottom of the tart shell. Arrange the grapes so they cover the tart shell in any pattern you wish. Brush the grapes with the remaining jam. Serve immediately or let stand at room temperature for up to 2 hours before serving.

1¼ cups all-purpose flour

⅓ cup walnut pieces

¼ cup packed light brown sugar

8 tablespoons (1 stick) unsalted butter, chilled and cut into 16 pieces

¼ cup smooth apricot, peach, or grape jam (use grape jam if using all red or purple grapes)

3 cups assorted colors small seedless grapes

TREASURE BOXES

4 SERVINGS

2 refrigerated folded pie crusts
  (15-ounce package)

¼ cup granulated sugar

1 tablespoon cornstarch

¼ cup orange juice

1 tablespoon lemon juice

2 tablespoons orange liqueur, such as
  Grand Marnier or Cointreau, or
  frozen orange juice concentrate,
  thawed

2 cups mixed bite-sized pieces of fruit

Preheat the oven to 400 degrees. Cut each pie crust in half. Ease the halves into four 4½-inch tart pans with removable bottoms. Trim the edges. Prick the bottoms several times with a fork. Place in the freezer for 5 minutes.

Bake the frozen crusts until golden and crisp, 12 to 14 minutes. Remove from the oven. (The pastry shells can be baked a day ahead and stored, covered, at room temperature.)

Meanwhile, combine the sugar and cornstarch in a medium saucepan. Gradually whisk in the orange and lemon juices. Stir constantly over medium heat until the mixture thickens and boils for 1 minute. Remove from the heat and stir in the liqueur or orange juice concentrate. Pour the filling into a mixing bowl and cool for 5 to 10 minutes. Gently stir the fruit into the filling to coat, then divide the coated fruit and filling among the tart shells. Refrigerate for at least 10 minutes or up to 3 hours before serving.

BANANA-MACADAMIA NUT TART

6 TO 8 SERVINGS

Preheat the oven to 425 degrees. Ease the pie crust into a 9-inch tart pan with a removable bottom, folding in the extra pastry to reinforce the edges. Prick the bottom of the pastry 8 or 10 times with a fork. Freeze the pastry in the pan for 10 minutes.

Bake the frozen crust until it is golden and crisp, 12 to 14 minutes. Let cool slightly. (The crust can be baked up to a day ahead and stored at room temperature.)

Shortly before serving, preheat the broiler. Grate 1 teaspoon of the colored part of the peel from the lemon and squeeze 1 tablespoon juice. In a small pan, heat the preserves with the butter, ginger, lemon peel, and juice until the butter is melted. Brush the baked tart shell with about 2 tablespoons of this glaze. Slice the bananas on a slight diagonal, then arrange in an overlapping pattern to cover the tart shell. Brush with the remaining glaze. Sprinkle with the macadamias.

Broil, 4 to 5 inches from the heat source, just until the topping is bubbly and the nuts are browned and fragrant, 1 to 2 minutes. Let cool for about 5 minutes, then serve immediately.

MACADAMIAS MAY BE THE most decadent nuts on the planet. Buttery and softly textured, they add a sophisticated accent to simple desserts such as this banana tart. Pineapple preserves and grated fresh ginger balance the richness of the nuts, and the bananas tie together all of the tropical Hawaiian flavors. The tart shell can be baked in advance, but the tart should be assembled and broiled shortly before serving so the bananas do not discolor.

1 refrigerated folded pie crust (half of a 15-ounce package)

1 lemon

¼ cup pineapple preserves

1 tablespoon unsalted butter

2 teaspoons grated fresh ginger

3 large, firm bananas, peeled

¼ cup coarsely chopped macadamia nuts

Orange Clove Tarts

6 SERVINGS

1 package (17 ounces) frozen puff
  pastry patty shells

6 small seedless oranges, peeled and
  cut crosswise into thin slices

5 tablespoons granulated sugar

2 teaspoons ground cloves

2 tablespoons unsalted butter, cut into
  small pieces

½ cup lemon or orange marmalade

1 tablespoon orange liqueur, such as
  Grand Marnier or Cointreau, or
  frozen orange juice concentrate,
  thawed

Preheat the oven to 400 degrees. On a lightly floured surface, roll each of the 6 pastry shells into a 6-inch circle. Place on a large baking sheet. Arrange the oranges in an overlapping circle on the pastry.

In a small dish, combine the sugar and cloves. Sprinkle each pastry and fruit with slightly less than 1 tablespoon of the clove sugar. Scatter the butter evenly on top of the fruit. Bake until the pastry is crisp and golden brown and the topping is bubbly, about 15 minutes.

Meanwhile, in a small pan, heat the marmalade with the liqueur or orange juice concentrate until melted. Brush over the baked tarts. Serve the tarts warm or at room temperature.

Wonton Flower Tartlets

MAKES 12 TARTLETS

WONTON SKINS AREN'T JUST for egg rolls. This "pastry" makes the easiest tart of all because it is already mixed, rolled, and cut for you. Pineapple preserves and cardamom provide a properly exotic filling, but I've used many other jam and spice combinations, as well as marzipan sprinkled with a few chopped almonds. The wonton skins can also be baked without any filling, then cooled and filled with melon-ball sized scoops of assorted sorbets for a refreshing, light dessert. You'll need miniature muffin tins, which are a low-cost, high-payoff kitchen investment.

Preheat the oven to 400 degrees. Brush both sides of the wonton skins with butter. (Be sure that you are using single skins—they often stick together in the package but are easy to separate.) Fit each into the cups of a miniature muffin tin, pressing gently to mold the skin to the cup. The tops of the wonton skins will extend to look somewhat like the petals of a flower.

In a small dish, combine the sugar and cardamom. Sprinkle the inside and the "petals" of the wontons with the spiced sugar. Fill each with about 1½ teaspoons of the preserves.

Bake until the tartlets are crisp, with dark golden edges, 6 to 7 minutes. Transfer the muffin tin to a rack and let the tartlets cool for a few minutes until they are firm. Gently pull on the petals to ease the tartlets out of the pan. Cool on a rack for at least 5 more minutes before serving warm or at room temperature. (The tartlets are best served within a few hours but can be stored in a tightly covered container for 1 day.)

12 (4-inch square) wonton skins

2 tablespoons unsalted butter, melted

1½ tablespoons granulated sugar

½ teaspoon ground cardamom

6 tablespoons pineapple preserves

APPLE MINCEMEAT TURNOVERS

MAKES 8 TURNOVERS

1⅓ cups prepared mincemeat

1 large tart apple, peeled and coarsely
chopped (about ¾ cup)

2 tablespoons dark rum

1 tablespoon grated orange peel

1½ teaspoons ground cinnamon

2 refrigerated folded pie crusts
(15-ounce package)

1 large egg, beaten with 2 teaspoons
water, for glaze

Preheat the oven to 425 degrees. In a medium bowl, stir together the mincemeat, apple, rum, orange peel, and cinnamon. Place the pie crusts on a work surface. Cut each into 4 wedges along the fold lines.

Place about ¼ cup of the mincemeat filling in the center of each wedge. Brush the egg glaze along the pastry edges. Fold the pastries in half lengthwise to form triangles; press the edges with the tines of a fork to seal them, then crimp decoratively. Arrange the turnovers on a large baking sheet. Cut 3 small slits in each with a sharp knife to allow steam to escape. Brush the tops of the pastry with more glaze.

Bake until golden and crisp, about 20 minutes. Serve warm or at room temperature.

GUAVA TURNOVERS

8 SERVINGS

Preheat the oven to 450 degrees. Cut the guava paste into 16 pieces. Lay both pie crusts on a lightly floured surface. Cut each into 4 wedges along the fold lines. On one side of each wedge, place 2 guava paste pieces, then sprinkle each with a pinch of cinnamon and about 1 teaspoon lime juice.

Wet your fingers and lightly moisten the edges of the turnovers. Fold the turnovers in half lengthwise to form triangles. Use the tines of a fork to crimp the edges. Use a knife to make 2 steam vent slashes in each turnover.

Arrange the turnovers on a large baking sheet. Bake until the edges are a rich golden brown and pastry is golden and crisp, 12 to 15 minutes. Use a spatula to transfer the turnovers to a rack to cool for at least 10 minutes before serving warm or at room temperature. (The turnovers are best served on the day of baking but can be frozen and gently reheated in a 350-degree oven before serving.)

Meanwhile, use a fork or whisk to blend the cream cheese with the powdered sugar and remaining lime juice (about 1 teaspoon). Serve each turnover with a dollop of whipped cream cheese.

GUAVA, A HIGHLY PERFUMED tropical fruit, is prized for its intense flavor. Guava paste, long a pantry staple in Latin American homes, has quietly made its way into ethnic markets and many supermarkets in the United States. Flaky pastry turnovers filled with guava paste are a breeze to make and are traditional throughout Latin America, where they are usually accompanied by a dollop of sweetened fresh, mild cheese similar to cream cheese.

12 ounces (about 1½ cups) guava paste

2 refrigerated folded pie crusts (15-ounce package)

1 teaspoon ground cinnamon

3 tablespoons lime juice

1 cup whipped cream cheese

3 tablespoons powdered sugar

CANDY

IF YOU THINK HOMEMADE CANDY ALWAYS INVOLVES LOTS OF TIME, EXPENSIVE PANS, special molds, thermometers, and frightening culinary terms like "couverture" or "tempering," think again. Some of the most delicious candies and confections—truffles, fudge, pralines, and even brittles—are easy and take practically no time to make.

It may be faster to buy a box of fancy wrapped chocolates, but nothing surpasses the charm of homemade candies, which are the perfect holiday or thank-you gift. A pan of fudge is a proven cure for stress—the results have been documented over several generations during exam time in college dorms. And a little doily-lined plate of truffles and a cup of coffee is the perfect dessert with any meal in any season. Because these candies can be made in minutes and store rather well, you can always keep them on hand.

There are no tricks or secrets to these recipes. They are simply streamlined versions of traditional recipes. A classic ganache, for example, which is nothing more than good chocolate melted in heavy cream, produces creamy truffles in minutes. With a basic formula and the right chocolate-to-cream proportions, you can endlessly vary these truffles with different types of chocolate, liqueur flavorings, and nuts, cocoa, or powdered sugar for coating.

Unlike traditional nut brittle and fudge, which come with recipe warnings about cooking to a precise temperature, Simple Peanut Brittle can be made in less than 10 minutes with no thermometer at all, and Classic Quick Fudge sets up in minutes—every time.

These candies, like all high-quality confections, will be only as good as the ingredients that go into them. Use the very best chocolate, butter, cream, and flavorings. Your candy will still be more economical than premium candy-store confections and will look and taste every bit as luscious, but with one critical difference: it will be homemade.

PEPPERED SESAME NUT CRUNCH

MAKES ABOUT 1 POUND

CHILI POWDER GIVES THIS candy a little kick, and if you double the amount, you can serve it as sweet-hot predinner hors d'oeuvre or snack with a glass of cold beer. As dessert, the crunch is particularly good crumbled and sprinkled over lemon or mango ice cream or sorbet.

Line a baking sheet with aluminum foil and butter the foil. In a medium saucepan over medium heat, stir the butter, brown sugar, corn syrup, and chili powder until melted, smooth, and bubbly. Cover and cook for 1 minute. Add the nuts and sesame seeds, raise the heat to medium-high, and cook, uncovered and stirring constantly, until the nuts are fragrant, lightly browned, and the syrup is dark golden, about 5 minutes.

Immediately pour the mixture onto the prepared baking sheet, spreading it thinly as quickly as possible. Cool for at least 15 minutes, then peel the candy away from the foil. Break it into pieces and serve. (The candy can be stored, tightly covered, at room temperature for up to 5 days.) When lukewarm, it will be a little chewy; when completely cool, it will be brittle.

4 tablespoons (½ stick) unsalted butter

½ cup packed light brown sugar

2 tablespoons light corn syrup

1 teaspoon chili powder

3 cups mixed salted nuts

2 tablespoons sesame seeds

1½ cups packed light brown sugar

1 cup half-and-half

1 tablespoon dark molasses

1½ cups pecan halves

FRENCH QUARTER PRALINES

MAKES ABOUT 18 PRALINES

Line a large baking sheet with foil and butter the foil generously. Combine the brown sugar, half-and-half, and molasses in a medium saucepan. Bring to a boil over medium heat, stirring to dissolve the sugar. After the mixture comes to a boil, cook for 12 minutes, stirring occasionally. Add the pecans and cook for 1 minute more.

Remove the pan from the heat. Let stand for 1 minute, then beat with a wooden spoon until the praline mixture cools slightly, thickens, and begins to pull away from the sides of the pan, 1 to 3 minutes. Quickly spoon the praline mixture by tablespoonfuls onto the prepared baking sheet.

Refrigerate the pralines on the baking sheet until they are firm enough to peel away, 10 to 15 minutes. Or cool at room temperature for at least 1 hour. (The pralines can be stored, tightly covered, in a cool place or in the refrigerator for up to 3 days.) They will remain chewy and soft like caramels, even when refrigerated.

SIMPLE PEANUT BRITTLE

MAKES ABOUT 1 POUND

Line a baking sheet with aluminum foil and butter the foil. In a medium saucepan over medium heat, stir the butter, sugar, and corn syrup until melted, smooth, and bubbly. Cover and cook for 1 minute. Stir in the nuts, raise the heat to medium-high and cook, stirring constantly, until the nuts are fragrant, lightly browned, and the syrup is dark golden, about 5 minutes.

Immediately pour the mixture onto the prepared baking sheet, spreading it thinly as quickly as possible. Cool for at least 15 minutes, then peel the candy away from the foil. Break it into pieces. (The brittle can be stored, tightly covered, at room temperature for up to 5 days.)

I'M ADDICTED TO PEANUT brittle. I like it plain, with fruit, crushed and stirred into chocolate or vanilla ice cream, sprinkled over pound cake, crushed and rolled around bananas, or even crumbled and topped with whipped cream. But most store-bought peanut brittle tastes stale, and most homemade recipes are intimidating and require a candy thermometer. This brittle cooks up in about 10 minutes, and it never fails. It's more peanuts than brittle, which is what makes it really good.

4 tablespoons (½ stick) unsalted butter

½ cup granulated sugar

2 tablespoons dark corn syrup

2 cups lightly salted small peanuts

CHOCOLATE THIN MINT TRIANGLES

MAKES 32 LARGE PIECES

12 ounces (2 cups) mint chocolate chips

6 ounces (1 cup) white chocolate chips

3-4 drops green food coloring

Line an 8-inch square baking pan with foil, allowing a 1-inch overhang on the sides. In a medium bowl set over simmering water or in a microwave oven, gently heat the mint chocolate chips until they are nearly melted (1½ to 2 minutes in a microwave, stopping to stir once or twice). Remove from the heat and stir until completely melted and smooth. Spread half the melted chocolate evenly over the bottom of the pan. Refrigerate until set, about 5 minutes.

Meanwhile, melt the white chocolate chips in the same way. Stir in enough food coloring so the mixture is mint green. Spread all the white chocolate over the layer of dark chocolate. Refrigerate until set, about 5 minutes. If the remaining dark chocolate has become too firm, heat gently to melt again. Spread the layer of dark chocolate over the white chocolate. Refrigerate until set, about 5 minutes.

Use the foil to remove the candy from the pan. Peel off the foil, use a small knife to trim the edges evenly, then cut the candy into sixteen 2-inch squares. Cut each square in half to make 32 triangles. Cool to room temperature before serving. (The mints can be refrigerated, covered, for up to 5 days or frozen for up to 1 month.)

CLASSIC QUICK FUDGE

MAKES 36 PIECES

In a small saucepan or in a bowl in a microwave oven, bring the condensed milk just to a boil. Place both of the chocolates in a medium mixing bowl. Pour the boiling milk over the chocolate and let stand for about 30 seconds, then stir gently until the chocolates are melted and the mixture is smooth. Stir in the vanilla and the walnuts, if desired.

Line an 8-inch square baking pan with aluminum foil, allowing a 1-inch overhang. Spread the fudge into the pan, smoothing the top. Place in the freezer until firm enough to cut, about 20 minutes. Or refrigerate at least 1 hour. Use the foil extensions to remove the fudge from the pan. Peel off the foil. Cut the fudge into 36 pieces. Serve immediately at a cool room temperature or slightly chilled. (The fudge can be refrigerated, covered, for up to 5 days or frozen for 1 month.)

I'VE BEEN MAKING CANDY FOR years. Still, I have only about a 50 percent track record for successful fudge from a traditional recipe. Cooking the sugar to just the right stage and keeping the mixture smooth is too tricky for me. But using condensed milk is a foolproof shortcut that bypasses the difficult boiling procedure because the canned milk has already been cooked with sugar to a smooth, silken consistency. You can double the recipe to use a whole can. The fudge will take a bit longer to set up in the refrigerator and the layer will be thicker, so you'll want to cut smaller pieces.

⅔ cup sweetened condensed milk (half of a 14-ounce can)

6 ounces (1 cup) semisweet chocolate chips

1 ounce unsweetened chocolate, chopped

1 teaspoon vanilla extract

½ cup chopped walnuts (optional)

MOLASSES TOOTSIES

MAKES 32 CANDIES

1 ounce unsweetened chocolate, chopped

1 tablespoon unsalted butter

¼ cup dark molasses

1 teaspoon vanilla extract

1 teaspoon ground ginger

1⅓-1½ cups powdered sugar

Line a baking sheet with waxed paper. In a small saucepan set over medium-low heat, stir the chocolate and butter until both are melted. Remove the pan from the heat and stir in the molasses, vanilla, and ginger until smooth. Add 1⅓ cups of the powdered sugar and blend with a wooden spoon until the mixture is stiff and smooth. If the dough remains too soft, knead in the remaining powdered sugar to form a stiff but malleable mixture.

Divide the mixture into 4 parts. Use your hands to shape each into a 10-inch log and set on the prepared baking sheet. Use a small sharp knife to cut each log into 8 pieces. Serve at a cool room temperature or slightly chilled. Or wrap each in a piece of waxed paper or plastic wrap, twisting the ends. (The tootsies can be refrigerated, covered, for up to 5 days or frozen for up to 1 month.)

WHIPPED CHOCOLATE TRUFFLES

MAKES ABOUT 30 TRUFFLES

TRUFFLES ARE AMONG THE easiest of candies to make but take a long time to mix. This technique ensures satisfaction in less than half an hour. The only caveat in an otherwise fail-safe recipe is to avoid overwhipping the chocolate mixture, which will make the truffles grainy. The procedure usually takes less than a minute, so watch carefully.

In a small saucepan, bring the cream just to a boil. Remove the pan from the heat and add the chocolate. Let stand about 30 seconds, then gently stir until the chocolate is melted and the mixture is smooth. (Return to low heat and stir for a minute or so if chocolate is not completely melted.) Stir in the liqueur or fruit syrup. Refrigerate the mixture, stirring every 5 minutes, until it is cool and beginning to thicken, 15 to 20 minutes.

Using an electric mixer, whip the chocolate mixture just until it holds soft peaks and becomes a shade lighter, 30 seconds to 1 minute. Refrigerate for about 5 minutes to firm it. Place the cocoa in a custard cup or small plastic bag. Shape walnut-sized pieces of the whipped chocolate mixture into rough nuggets and roll or toss them in the cocoa to coat completely. Let the truffles dry on a piece of waxed paper for about 5 minutes, then serve. (The truffles can be refrigerated, covered, for up to 5 days or frozen for 1 month.) They have their fullest flavor when served at a cool room temperature.

⅓ cup heavy cream

6 ounces (1 cup) semisweet chocolate chips or bittersweet chocolate, chopped

1 tablespoon cognac or other liqueur of choice, or fruit syrup

3 tablespoons unsweetened cocoa, preferably European-style

WHITE TRUFFLES

MAKES ABOUT 24 TRUFFLES

8 ounces (1⅓ cups) white chocolate chips or white chocolate, chopped

¼ cup crème fraîche, at room temperature

2 teaspoons rose water

½ teaspoon ground cardamom

½ cup finely chopped almonds

In a medium bowl set over a pan of simmering water or in a microwave oven, gently heat the chocolate until it is nearly melted (about 1 minute in a microwave). Remove from the heat and stir until smooth. Stir in the crème fraîche, rosewater, and cardamom until smooth. Refrigerate or place in the freezer, stirring once or twice, until cool and thickened, about 15 minutes.

Meanwhile, toast the almonds in a dry skillet over medium-high heat, stirring, until golden and fragrant, about 3 minutes. (Or toast on a baking sheet in a 350-degree oven, stirring occasionally, for 5 to 10 minutes.) Let cool for at least 5 minutes.

Pinch off and form the truffle mixture into walnut-sized balls. Roll each truffle in the nuts to coat. Let the truffles dry on a piece of waxed paper for at least 5 minutes. (The truffles can be refrigerated, covered, for up to 5 days or frozen for 1 month.) Serve slightly chilled or at a cool room temperature.

CHOCOLATE HAZELNUT TRUFFLES

MAKES ABOUT 24 TRUFFLES

NUTELLA, A CHOCOLATE-hazelnut spread that Italians favor as much as Americans do peanut butter, is now sold in supermarkets in the peanut butter section. Its nutty chocolate flavor enriches these simple confections, and its thick, smooth texture firms them as soon as it is stirred into the melted chocolate and cream, forming a nearly instant truffle.

In a medium bowl set over a pan of simmering water or in a microwave oven, gently heat the chocolate until it is nearly melted (1 to 1½ minutes in a microwave). Remove from the heat and stir gently until smooth. Stir in the Nutella until smooth, then stir in the cream. The mixture will thicken almost immediately. Refrigerate, stirring once or twice, until it is cooled and thickens further to a truffle consistency, 5 to 10 minutes.

In a food processor, pulse the hazelnuts once or twice until finely chopped. Place them in a shallow dish. Pinch off and form the truffle mixture into walnut-sized balls. Roll each truffle in the nuts to coat. Let the truffles dry on a piece of waxed paper for at least 5 minutes. (The truffles can be refrigerated, covered, for up to 5 days or frozen for 1 month.) Serve at a cool room temperature.

8 ounces bittersweet chocolate, chopped

¼ cup Nutella or other chocolate-hazelnut spread

3 tablespoons heavy cream

½ cup chopped skinned hazelnuts (see page 34)

"COCONUTS"

MAKES ABOUT 24 TRUFFLES

2 ounces (⅓ cup) white chocolate chips

1½ cups shredded sweetened coconut

1½ cups powdered sugar

3 tablespoons sour cream

¼ teaspoon almond extract

¼ cup unsweetened cocoa, preferably European-style

In a small bowl set over simmering water or in a microwave oven, gently heat the white chocolate until nearly melted (about 30 seconds in a microwave). Remove from the heat and stir until smooth. Let cool for a few minutes.

Meanwhile, in a food processor, process the coconut and powdered sugar until the coconut is finely chopped. Add the sour cream, almond extract, and melted white chocolate. Process just until blended. Refrigerate the mixture, stirring once or twice, until cool and thick, about 15 minutes.

Place the cocoa in a shallow dish or small sturdy plastic bag. Pinch off and form the truffle mixture into walnut-sized balls. Roll or shake each truffle in cocoa to coat completely. Let the truffles dry on a piece of waxed paper for at least 5 minutes. (The truffles can be refrigerated, covered, for up to 5 days or frozen for 1 month.) Serve at a cool room temperature.

GUAVA TRUFFLES

MAKES ABOUT 24 TRUFFLES

In a medium bowl set over a pan of simmering water or in a microwave oven, gently heat the white chocolate and cream until the chocolate is nearly melted (1 to 1½ minutes in a microwave). Remove from the heat and stir until melted. Stir in the guava paste and rum until smooth. Refrigerate, stirring once or twice, until cool and thickened, about 15 minutes.

Meanwhile, toast the coconut in a dry skillet over medium heat, stirring, until tinged with brown and fragrant, 2 to 3 minutes. (Or toast on a small baking sheet in a 375-degree oven for 3 to 5 minutes, stirring occasionally.) Cool for at least 5 minutes.

Place the toasted coconut in a shallow dish. Pinch off and form the truffle mixture into walnut-sized balls. Roll each truffle in the coconut to coat. Let the truffles dry on a piece of waxed paper for at least 5 minutes. (The truffles can be refrigerated, covered, for up to 5 days or frozen for 1 month.) Serve at a cool room temperature.

8 ounces (1⅓ cups) white chocolate chips or white chocolate, chopped

2 tablespoons heavy cream

½ cup (4 ounces) guava paste

2 teaspoons dark rum

½ cup shredded sweetened coconut

1½ cups (6-ounce package) mixed chopped dried fruits

½ cup slivered almonds

2 tablespoons brandy or bourbon, or orange juice

½ teaspoon grated nutmeg, preferably freshly grated

3 tablespoons granulated sugar

SUGARPLUMS

MAKES ABOUT 20

In a food processor, finely chop the fruits and almonds together. Add the liquor or orange juice and nutmeg. Process just until the mixture is finely ground and sticks together, 10 to 15 seconds.

Place the sugar on a small plate. Line a tray with waxed paper. Dip your fingers in the sugar, then pinch off and form ¾-to-1-inch balls of the fruit-nut mixture. Roll each in the sugar to coat, then set on the prepared tray to dry for at least 10 minutes, and serve. (The sugarplums can be refrigerated, covered, for up to 1 week or frozen for 1 month.)

INDEX

Honey Nectarine Cheesecake, 114

Lemon Blueberry Cloud, 113

Peanut Butter, 117

Raspberry–White Chocolate Demitasse, 116

Mulled-Wine Syrup, Clementines in, 39

N

Nectarine Honey Cheesecake Mousse, 114

Nectarines, Grilled Pound Cake with, 57; variations, 57

No-Bake Ginger-Orange Cheesecake, 189

Nut(s). *See also* Name of nut

Bars, Pine, and Tuscan Rosemary, 152

Crunch, Peppered Sesame, 217

and fruits, care of, 16

Honey Shortbreads, 151

Nutmeg Butter Balls, 162

Nutmeg Crumb Cake, 173

O

Oat-Maple Bourbon Balls, 153

Oatmeal Peach Trifle, 125

Oatmeal Plum Crisp, 60

Orange. *See also* Citrus

Clove Tarts, 210; variations, 210

-Cranberry Bars, 158

-Cranberry Sundaes, 95

Custard, Strawberries in, 119

-Ginger Cheesecake, No-Bake, 189

and Grapefruit Compote with Candied Zest, 40

P

Palermo Parfaits (biscotti, chocolate, dried fruits), 98

Panini, Peanut Butter, with Concord Grapes, 70

pantry (items) basic, for baking, 13

Papaya(s)

Calypso Kabobs, 71

Key West Sunsets, 91

and Kiwis, Sliced, with Rum Sauce, 43

Peppered Pineapple, 44

Parfaits. *See* Ice Cream

Pastina Pudding, Nana's, 142

Pavlovas, Personal, 127

Peach(es)

-Citrus Soufflés, 145; variations, 145

Crunch, Broiled, 55

Kissel, Blushing, 112

Oatmeal Trifle, 125, 125

Pureed, and Fresh Raspberry Coupe, 87

Roasted, with Pound Cake and Pistachio Ice Cream, 56

Peanut Brittle, Simple, 219

Peanut Butter

Banana-Raisin Cookies, 168

Mousse, 117

Panini with Concord Grapes, 70

Pear(s)

about chilling, 36; about poaching, 37

Almond Galette, 205; variation, with apple, 205

Bittersweet Chocolate Mousse with, 115; variations, 115

Cool Poached, with Shaved Chocolate, 37

Mincemeat Turnovers, 212

with Pecorino and Pepper, 36

Roasted, with Amaretti Crumble, 63

Seckel, Tea-Poached, 64

Pecan Tart, Southern, 206

Pecorino and Pepper, Pears with, 36

Peppered Pineapple Papayas, 44

Peppered Sesame Nut Crunch, 217

pie crusts, 200. *See also* Tarts

Pignoli (pine nut) Macaroons, Italian, 165

Pine Nut Bars, Tuscan Rosemary and, 152

Pineapple

-Citrus Salad, Southern, 38

Maui Madness (with macadamia nuts and coffee ice cream), 94

Papayas, Peppered, 44

Right-Side-Up Pound Cake, 191